W9-AHB-564

STEPPING
STONES
SU*to*CCESS

EXPERTS SHARE STRATEGIES
FOR MASTERING BUSINESS,
LIFE, & RELATIONSHIPS

*With much
Kindness,
Samy
Dec '09*

Stepping Stones to Success
Copyright © 2009

Published in the United States by
INSIGHT PUBLISHING
Sevierville, Tennessee • www.insightpublishing.com

All rights reserved. No part of this book may be
reproduced in any form or by any means without prior
written permission from the publisher except for brief
quotations embodied in critical essay, article, or review.
These articles and/or reviews must state the correct title
and contributing authors of this book by name.

Disclaimer: This book is a compilation of ideas from
numerous experts who have each contributed a chapter.
As such, the views expressed in each chapter are of those
who were interviewed and not necessarily of the
interviewer, Insight Publishing or the other contributing
authors.

Table of Contents

A Message from the Publisher

There are many things I've come to understand throughout the many years I have been in this business. I've learned that it's never too late to grow and learn, to change course, to expand perspectives, and to admit I don't know everything.

Because I know it's important to learn from the experience of others, I reached out to many experts when putting this book project together and I gained some valuable information from them. The people I talked with have presented some insights that will expand your horizons and make you realize that you can be the key to your own success.

This book, *Stepping Stones to Success,* is your golden opportunity to profit from the knowledge of others. It will give you the facts you need to make important decisions about your future.

Interviewing these fascinating people was a unique learning experience for me. And I assure you that reading this book will be an exceptional learning experience for you.

—David Wright

The interviews presented in
Stepping Stones to Success
are conducted by David Wright,
President and Founder of
International Speakers Network
and Insight Publishing.

CHAPTER ONE

Powerful Leadership Qualities

DAVID WRIGHT (WRIGHT)

Today we are talking with Frank Prince; President and Founder of Unleash Your Mind, a consulting firm whose mission is to unlock innovative thinking within organizations. Frank's mantra, "stop talking about it and start doing it," is not only what he teaches but what he lives as he travels the world sparking innovation in businesses and individuals. Recognized as a global leader in the field of creativity, Frank is a popular keynote speaker. He is the author of seven books and numerous articles. His bestseller, *C and the Box*, has been described as an elegant approach to paradigm shift thinking and has helped thousands learn to look at their life situations creatively. Along with Stephen Covey (*7 Habits of Highly Effective People*) and Ken Blanchard (*The one Minute manager*) Frank co-authored the book, *Blueprint for Success.* Frank turns businesses into idea factories as he conducts workshops in creative problem solving, customer focus sales, and leadership. He also facilitates strategic planning sessions for the executive teams of several Fortune 100 companies. These sessions concentrate on driving top and bottom line growth over the ensuing year through implementation of innovation.

After years of studying creativity at a subconscious level, Frank has developed two products targeted at the subconscious mind. *Speed Sleep* is an audio recording that both accelerate sleep and jump starts the brains incubation process. This incubation process can help us solve problems literally while we sleep. *Thought Free Golf* is an instructional book and CD system that provides the listener skills to master the mental side of the game of golf.

Frank welcome to *Stepping Stones to Success*.

FRANK PRINCE (PRINCE)
Thank you.

WRIGHT
You work with the leadership of several Fortune 100 companies. What is it that makes them so successful? What are they doing differently?

PRINCE
One of the things I have noticed is that the leaders of successful companies have learned to make a distinction between leadership and what I call "managership." Being a leader involves things like having the ability to develop one on one rapport with employees and clients, developing willing followership, and establishing mutual goals. On the other hand, managership has to do with things like planning, organizing, directing, and controlling. You need both leadership and managership in organizations. The problem comes when the top executives of companies find themselves managing instead of leading.

Lately I have been researching examples of exceptional leaders in history. One such leader, Sir Ernest Shackleton, and the story of his voyage to the Antarctic provides a powerful picture of the kind of leadership that leads to success.

Let me take a moment to tell you his story: Shackleton's boat, The Endurance, left for Antarctica in December of 1914. There were twenty-eight men, including Shackleton on board. After crossing icy seas to the Antarctic, he planned to lead his men on the first ever dog sled expedition across the frozen continent. But in mid January, just a day away from their desired landfall, the ship became trapped in sea ice. No one knew where they were and few were bold enough to sail those seas anyway. Shackleton's team was forced to winter with The Endurance stuck in the ice. They survived ten cold months awaiting the spring thaw to free the boat but instead of setting them free the melting caused the ice to move, putting a great deal of pressure on the ship's hull. Sadly, the men watched the ice slowly crush the vessel that they had learned to call home. Forced to abandon ship, the crew camped on an ice pack for five more months hoping the ice flow itself would drift toward land. They knew of an island located about 250 miles away.

On April 9, 1916, the ice floe broke apart and Shackleton ordered the men to the lifeboats that they salvaged from their beloved ship. They started rowing toward what they had figured was the closest land. After seven freezing days at sea the men landed on the inhospitable shore of Elephant Island, where sadly they knew that no one would think to search for them. When it looked like they would run out of food and courage before anyone would come, Shackleton decided to make an open boat journey to go for help. This journey would be a treacherous eight-hundred-mile icy ocean crossing to South Georgia Island. To make it he would have to leave twenty-two of his men behind. This harrowing fifteen-day trip in a makeshift sailboat built from the life boats, is now considered one of the greatest boat journeys in history. Together the crew of five faced fifty-foot waves and gale force winds. Finally they were able to land but not before encountering a hurricane that forced them to land on the opposite side of the island from the whaling station where they were counting on finding help. Due to damage to their lifeboat, the only way to reach the station was to cross the island over six-thousand-foot ice covered mountains. But determined to rescue the twenty-two men he had to leave on Elephant Island, Shackleton and two of the others who had made the ocean crossing, set out leaving the other two men at the landing point. After thirty-six hours of climbing, sliding and trekking across some of the most challenging terrain on Earth, on May 20, 1916, they reached the island's remote whaling station. They were the first men ever to cross South Georgia island.

Immediately Shackleton organized a rescue team to save the men on the other side of South Georgia Island. Then, over the next three months he made numerous attempts through stormy seas to reach Elephant Island to rescue the other twenty-two men. It was four and half months since those men had last seen their captain, and almost all hope was gone. Finally, on August 30, 1916, Shackleton made it back to Elephant Island and was able to rescue the men he had left behind. Nearly two years had passed on this incredible journey, and against all odds, not a life from the Endurance was lost.

As I spend time working with business leaders, Sir Earnest Shackleton's story inspires me to ask: Do these men and women have leadership qualities similar to Shackleton's? Have they been able to develop the kind of rapport and respect with their "crews" that he did? Are the people they lead following them willingly toward clearly established mutual goals?

WRIGHT

You keep mentioning developing rapport. How do successful leaders develop rapport with their employees?

PRINCE

People who understand leadership, understand that they need the ability to quickly develop rapport with others. Matching and pacing others are two ways to build rapport. By being able to let go of yourself and then focusing on others, you can learn to understand them. This is the quickest way to develop rapport.

Earnest Shackleton's men called him, The Boss, but they called him The Boss totally out of respect and not out of fear. He knew his men very well. He made a point to spend time with each of them individually, learning what was important to them. Business leaders could learn from Shackleton's ways of building rapport.

WRIGHT

You also talked about "willing followership" as a leadership trait. What is the secret to developing willing followers?

PRINCE

New supervisors, especially college recruits, often come into their careers believing that it is their job to tell their direct reports what to do. It doesn't take the smart ones too long to see that the workers already know what to do. The real job of a supervisor is to remove obstacles so the workers can get their jobs done. It is easy for leaders to develop "willing followership" if they are willing to do what they are asking those under them to do. Shackleton is a great example of leading by doing. He boarded that tiny boat to cross the boiling sea with his men. He put nails in his boots so he could trek across the ice to the whaling station. He didn't send the others and stay behind. He was willing to do every task he expected his crew members to do, and he never hesitated to take the lead even when that meant breaking the trail, which was the most strenuous position in the line.

WRIGHT

The third leadership trait you mentioned was establishing mutual goals, most companies take the time to sit down and write out their goals, what's different in a successful company's approach?

PRINCE

People sign up to work for an organization for a reason. They take a job because they have a need and that need isn't always purely financial. Some organizations get clear on their goals and measure them quite frequently. Successful organizations take the next step and look at how the company's goals match up with the employee's needs. When a business's needs and goals are in alignment with the individual's needs and goals, the employees are highly motivated and the company becomes an exciting place to work.

People support what they help to create. Goals become powerful if the people within an organization have a part in establishing them. Shackleton was strong in terms of goal communication. His crew understood when they boarded the Endurance that the first goal of the expedition was to cross the Antarctic by dog sled. However, after they ended up having to abandon the ship and use the supplies they had packed for the sled trip to survive the winter, the goal changed. It was at this point that Shackleton made it clear that the new goal was for every man to return safely. This goal was bravely achieved.

Shackleton valued adventure, but he valued the lives of his men more. Our values are at the core of what motivates us.

WRIGHT

What role do values play in success?

PRINCE

When people are fortunate enough to work for an organization that has similar values to their own they usually thrive and have a much higher chance of being successful. Unfortunately, however, individuals don't often stop and take the time to ask themselves the question, What is most important to me? And an even better question would be, "What is most important to me this year?" It is a fact, our values change over time. Events such as marriage, the birth of a child, or an illness can all affect what we view as most important. If you don't believe me talk to someone who's had a heart attack. Almost without exception you'll find that the value of good health has moved right to the top of their list.

WRIGHT

What role do values play in leadership?

PRINCE

Understanding people's values can often help us better understand their strengths. Successful leaders are all about utilizing their team member's strengths. Unfortunately, most organizations assessments or personal development plans end up with action plans developed around an individual's weaknesses. While we certainly need to be aware of our weaknesses, it is much more productive to take the time to understand our strengths well enough to leverage them. The keys to an organization getting the right people in the right place are: 1. To understand other people's values, and 2. To recognize their strengths. When employees are put in a job where they can do what they believe in, and do what they do best, they will not only enjoy their work but will contribute mightily to the success of the organization.

WRIGHT

The story of Shackleton's Antarctic adventure sounds like an amazing demonstration of successful leadership. He demonstrated many of the skills that you've talked about here today. It must have been incredible for his men to experience that level of leadership?

PRINCE

Yes, as a matter of fact, the leaders I work with often talk about how the toughest challenges they have faced in the past influence the way they lead people today. Leaders who have made it to the peak or to the top of an organization, often reference hardships, challenging assignments, or even failures as the things that make them the strong leaders they are today.

There is one last leadership trait that I'd like to mention and that is "heart." Shackleton was known as a man with heart. He was a fierce, determined warrior but he was also pretty in touch with his emotions. A strong leader has to have heart to communicate a vision. He has to believe in a cause enough to be willing to put himself and his reputation on the line. And he has to have enough passion to be able to convince others to go on the journey with him.

Perhaps one of the greatest leaders of all time, Sir Ernest Shackleton, was able to hold his crew together, give them strength to persevere, motivate them to action, make sure they understood their goal and inspire them to continue to believe, against all odds, that not one of them would be lost.

WRIGHT

Well Frank, I really appreciate you taking this time to share your ideas on leadership. I've learned a lot today and I'm sure our readers will as well.

PRINCE

It was my pleasure.

WRIGHT

Today, we've been talking with Frank Prince; Frank takes a no nonsense approach to implementing innovation within organizations. Since 1988 he has focused his work on delivering skills such as leadership, creativity and strategic planning to individuals in the business world. These skills have proven again and again to drive top line sales and bottom line results. How does he do it? By tapping into the most underused resource that exists in business today; the minds of people.

Working at all levels in organizations, Frank gives up front sales people creative problem solving skills that can be used to institute a customer oriented sales force. He works with middle management to evolve their skills from "managership" to leadership. He also works with senior executives designing and developing idea factories that drive the innovation and positive change that will ensure success in the future.

Frank, thanks again for being with us today on *Stepping Stones to Success*.

FRANK PRINCE is President and Founder of Unleash Your Mind, a consulting firm whose mission is to unlock innovative thinking within organizations. Frank's mantra "stop talking about it and start doing it" is not only what he teaches but what he lives as he travels the world sparking innovation in businesses and individuals. Recognized as a global leader in the field of creativity, Frank is a popular keynote speaker. He is the author of 7 books; and numerous articles. His best seller, C and the Box, has been described as an elegant approach to paradigm shift thinking and has helped thousands learn to look at their life situations creatively. Along with Stephen Covey (*7 Habits of Highly Effective People*) and Ken Blanchard (*The One Minute Manager*) Frank co-authored the book, *Blueprint for Success*. Frank turns businesses into idea factories as he conducts workshops in creative problem solving, customer focus sales, and leadership. He also facilitates strategic planning sessions for the executive teams of several Fortune 100 companies. These sessions concentrate on driving top and bottom line growth over the ensuing year through implementation of innovation.

After years of studying creativity at a subconscious level, Frank has developed two products targeted at the subconscious mind. Speed Sleep is an audio recording that both accelerate sleep and jump starts the brains incubation process. This incubation process can help us solve problems literally while we sleep. Thought Free Golf is an instructional book and CD system that provides the listener skills to master the mental side of the game of golf.

FRANK A. PRINCE

16304 Rock Lake Drive
Odessa, Florida 33556
214-215-8555
frankprince@mindspring.com
www.FrankPrince.com
www.SpeedSleep.com
www.ThoughtFreeGolf.com

CHAPTER TWO

Find a Mentor and Believe in Your Dreams

AN INTERVIEW WITH.... JACK CANFIELD

DAVID WRIGHT (WRIGHT)

Today we are talking with Jack Canfield. You probably know him as the founder and co-creator of the *New York Times* number one bestselling *Chicken Soup for the Soul* book series. As of 2006 there are sixty-five titles and eighty million copies in print in over thirty-seven languages.

Jack's background includes a BA from Harvard, a master's from the University of Massachusetts, and an Honorary Doctorate from the University of Santa Monica. He has been a high school and university teacher, a workshop facilitator, a psychotherapist, and a leading authority in the area of self-esteem and personal development.

Jack Canfield, welcome to *Stepping Stones to Success.*

JACK CANFIELD (CANFIELD)

Thank you, David. It's great to be with you.

WRIGHT

When I talked with Mark Victor Hansen, he gave you full credit for coming up with the idea of the *Chicken Soup* series. Obviously it's made you an internationally known personality. Other than recognition, has the series changed you personally and if so, how?

CANFIELD

I would say that it has and I think in a couple of ways. Number one, I read stories all day long of people who've overcome what would feel like insurmountable obstacles. For example, we just did a book *Chicken Soup for the Unsinkable Soul*. There's a story in there about a single mother with three daughters. She contracted a disease and she had to have both of her hands and both of her feet amputated. She got prosthetic devices and was able to learn how to use them. She could cook, drive the car, brush her daughters' hair, get a job, etc. I read that and I thought, "God, what would I ever have to complain and whine and moan about?"

At one level it's just given me a great sense of gratitude and appreciation for everything I have and it has made me less irritable about the little things.

I think the other thing that's happened for me personally is my sphere of influence has changed. By that I mean I was asked, for example, some years ago to be the keynote speaker to the Women's Congressional Caucus. The Caucus is a group that includes all women in America who are members of Congress and who are state senators, governors, and lieutenant governors. I asked what they wanted me to talk about—what topic.

"Whatever you think we need to know to be better legislators," was the reply.

I thought, "Wow, they want me to tell them about what laws they should be making and what would make a better culture." Well, that wouldn't have happened if our books hadn't come out and I hadn't become famous. I think I get to play with people at a higher level and have more influence in the world. That's important to me because my life purpose is inspiring and empowering people to live their highest vision so the world works for everybody. I get to do that on a much bigger level than when I was just a high school teacher back in Chicago.

WRIGHT

I think one of the powerful components of that book series is that you can read a positive story in just a few minutes and come back and revisit it. I know my daughter has three of the books and she just reads them interchangeably. Sometimes I go in her bedroom and she'll be crying and reading one of them. Other times she'll be laughing, so they really are "chicken soup for the soul," aren't they?

CANFIELD

They really are. In fact we have four books in the *Teenage Soul* series now and a new one coming out at the end of this year. I have a son who's eleven and he has a twelve-year-old friend who's a girl. We have a new book called *Chicken Soup for the Teenage Soul and the Tough Stuff*. It's all about dealing with parents' divorces, teachers who don't understand you, boyfriends who drink and drive, and other issues pertinent to that age group.

I asked my son's friend, "Why do you like this book?" (It's our most popular book among teens right now.) She said, "You know, whenever I'm feeling down I read it and it makes me cry and I feel better. Some of the stories make me laugh and some of the stories make me feel more responsible for my life. But basically I just feel like I'm not alone."

One of the people I work with recently said that the books are like a support group between the covers of a book — you can read about other peoples' experiences and realize you're not the only one going through something.

WRIGHT

Jack, we're trying to encourage people in our audience to be better, to live better, and be more fulfilled by reading about the experiences of our writers. Is there anyone or anything in your life that has made a difference for you and helped you to become a better person?

CANFIELD

Yes, and we could do ten books just on that. I'm influenced by people all the time. If I were to go way back I'd have to say one of the key influences in my life was Jesse Jackson when he was still a minister in Chicago. I was teaching in an all black high school there and I went to Jesse Jackson's church with a friend one time. What happened for me was that I saw somebody with a vision. (This was before Martin Luther King was killed and Jesse was of the lieutenants in his organization.) I just saw people trying to make the world work better for a certain segment of the population. I was inspired by that kind of visionary belief that it's possible to make change.

Later on, John F. Kennedy was a hero of mine. I was very much inspired by him.

Another is a therapist by the name of Robert Resnick. He was my therapist for two years. He taught me a little formula: E + R = O. It stands for Events + Response = Outcome. He said, "If you don't like your outcomes quit blaming the events and start changing your responses." One of his favorite phrases was, "If the grass on the other side of the fence looks greener, start watering your own lawn more."

I think he helped me get off any kind of self-pity I might have had because I had parents who were alcoholics. It would have been very easy to blame them for problems I might have had. They weren't very successful or rich; I was surrounded by people who were and I felt like, "God, what if I'd had parents like they had? I could have been a lot better." He just got me off that whole notion and made me realize that the hand you were dealt is the hand you've got to play. Take responsibility for who you are and quit complaining and blaming others and get on with your life. That was a turning point for me.

I'd say the last person who really affected me big-time was a guy named W. Clement Stone who was a self-made multi-millionaire in Chicago. He taught me that success is not a four-letter word—it's nothing to be ashamed of—and you ought to go for it. He said, "The best thing you can do for the poor is not be one of them." Be a model for what it is to live a successful life. So I learned from him the principles of success and that's what I've been teaching now for more than thirty years.

WRIGHT

He was an entrepreneur in the insurance industry, wasn't he?

CANFIELD

He was. He had combined insurance. When I worked for him he was worth 600 million dollars and that was before the dot.com millionaires came along in Silicon Valley. He just knew more about success. He was a good friend of Napoleon Hill (author of *Think and Grow Rich)* and he was a fabulous mentor. I really learned a lot from him.

WRIGHT

I miss some of the men I listened to when I was a young salesman coming up and he was one of them. Napoleon Hill was another one as was Dr. Peale. All of their writings made me who I am today. I'm glad I had that opportunity.

CANFIELD

One speaker whose name you probably will remember, Charlie "Tremendous" Jones, says, "Who we are is a result of the books we read and the people we hang out with." I think that's so true and that's why I tell people, "If you want to have high self-esteem, hang out with people who have high self-esteem. If you want to be more spiritual, hang out with spiritual people." We're always telling our children, "Don't hang out with those kids." The reason we don't want them to is because we know how influential people are with each other. I think we need to give ourselves the same advice. Who are we hanging out with? We can hang out with them in books, cassette tapes, CDs, radio shows, and in person.

WRIGHT

One of my favorites was a fellow named Bill Gove from Florida. I talked with him about three or four years ago. He's retired now. His mind is still as quick as it ever was. I thought he was one of the greatest speakers I had ever heard.

What do you think makes up a great mentor? In other words, are there characteristics that mentors seem to have in common?

CANFIELD

I think there are two obvious ones. I think mentors have to have the time to do it and the willingness to do it. I also think they need to be people who are doing something you want to do. W. Clement Stone used to tell me, "If you want to be rich, hang out with rich people. Watch what they do, eat what they eat, dress the way they dress—try it on." He wasn't suggesting that you give up your authentic self, but he was pointing out that rich people probably have habits that you don't have and you should study them.

I always ask salespeople in an organization, "Who are the top two or three in your organization?" I tell them to start taking them out to lunch and dinner and for a drink and finding out what they do. Ask them, "What's your secret?" Nine times out of ten they'll be willing to tell you.

This goes back to what we said earlier about asking. I'll go into corporations and I'll say, "Who are the top ten people?" They'll all tell me and I'll say, "Did you ever ask them what they do different than you?"

"No," they'll reply.

"Why not?"

"Well, they might not want to tell me."

"How do you know? Did you ever ask them? All they can do is say no. You'll be no worse off than you are now."

So I think with mentors you just look at people who seem to be living the life you want to live and achieving the results you want to achieve.

What we say in our book is when that you approach a mentor they're probably busy and successful and so they haven't got a lot of time. Just ask, "Can I talk to you for ten minutes every month?" If I know it's only going to be ten minutes I'll probably say yes. The neat thing is if I like you I'll always give you more than ten minutes, but that ten minutes gets you in the door.

WRIGHT

In the future are there any more Jack Canfield books authored singularly?

CANFIELD

One of my books includes the formula I mentioned earlier: $E + R = O$. I just felt I wanted to get that out there because every time I give a speech and I talk about that the whole room gets so quiet you could hear a pin drop—I can tell people are really getting value.

Then I'm going to do a series of books on the principles of success. I've got about 150 of them that I've identified over the years. I have a book down the road I want to do that's called *No More Put-Downs*, which is a book probably aimed mostly at parents, teachers, and managers. There's a culture we have now of put-down humor. Whether it's *Married . . . with Children* or *All in the Family*, there's that characteristic of macho put-down humor. There's research now showing how bad it is for kids' self-esteem when the coaches do it, so I want to get that message out there as well.

WRIGHT

It's really not that funny, is it?

CANFIELD

No, we'll laugh it off because we don't want to look like we're a wimp but underneath we're hurt. The research now shows that you're better off breaking a child's bones than you are breaking his or her spirit. A bone will heal much more quickly than their emotional spirit will.

WRIGHT

I remember recently reading a survey where people listed the top five people who had influenced them. I've tried it on a couple of groups at church and in other places. In my case, and in the survey, approximately three out of the top five are always teachers. I wonder if that's going to be the same in the next decade.

CANFIELD

I think that's probably because as children we're at our most formative years. We actually spend more time with our teachers than we do with our parents. Research shows that the average parent only interacts verbally with each of their children only about eight and a half minutes a day. Yet at school they're interacting with their teachers for anywhere from six to eight hours depending on how long the school day is, including coaches, chorus directors, etc.

I think that in almost everybody's life there's been that one teacher who loved him or her as a human being—an individual—not just one of the many students the teacher was supposed to fill full of History and English. That teacher believed in you and inspired you.

Les Brown is one of the great motivational speakers in the world. If it hadn't been for one teacher who said, "I think you can do more than be in a special education class. I think you're the one," he'd probably still be cutting grass in the median strip of the highways in Florida instead of being a $35,000-a-talk speaker.

WRIGHT

I had a conversation one time with Les. He told me about this wonderful teacher who discovered Les was dyslexic. Everybody else called him dumb and this one lady just took him under her wing and had him tested. His entire life changed because of her interest in him.

CANFIELD

I'm on the board of advisors of the Dyslexic Awareness Resource Center here in Santa Barbara. The reason is because I taught high school and had a lot of kids who were called "at-risk"—kids who would end up in gangs and so forth.

What we found over and over was that about 78 percent of all the kids in the juvenile detention centers in Chicago were kids who had learning disabilities—primarily dyslexia—but there were others as well. They were never diagnosed and they weren't doing well in school so they'd drop out. As soon as a student drops out of school he or she becomes subject to the influence of gangs and other kinds of criminal and drug linked activities. If these kids had been diagnosed earlier we'd have been able to get rid of a large amount of the juvenile crime in America because there are a lot of really good programs that can teach dyslexics to read and excel in school.

WRIGHT

My wife is a teacher and she brings home stories that are heartbreaking about parents not being as concerned with their children as they used to be, or at least not as helpful as they used to be. Did you find that to be a problem when you were teaching?

CANFIELD

It depends on what kind of district you're in. If it's a poor district the parents could be on drugs, alcoholics, and basically just not available. If you're in a really high rent district the parents are not available because they're both working, coming home tired, they're jet-setters, or they're working late at the office because they're workaholics. Sometimes it just legitimately takes two paychecks to pay the rent anymore.

I find that the majority of parents care but often they don't know what to do. They don't know how to discipline their children. They don't know how to help them with their homework. They can't pass on skills that they never acquired themselves.

Unfortunately, the trend tends to be like a chain letter. The people with the least amount of skills tend to have the most number of children. The other thing is that you get crack babies (infants born addicted to crack cocaine because of the mother's addiction). As of this writing, in Los Angeles one out of every ten babies born is a crack baby.

WRIGHT

That's unbelievable.

CANFIELD

Yes, and another statistic is that by the time 50 percent of the kids are twelve years old they have started experimenting with alcohol. I see a lot of that in the Bible belt. The problem is not the big city, urban designer drugs, but alcoholism.

Another thing you get, unfortunately, is a lot of let's call it "familial violence" — kids getting beat up, parents who drink and then explode, child abuse, and sexual abuse. You see a lot of that.

WRIGHT

Most people are fascinated by these television shows about being a survivor. What has been the greatest comeback that you have made from adversity in your career or in your life?

CANFIELD

You know, it's funny, I don't think I've had a lot of major failures and setbacks where I had to start over. My life's been on an intentional curve. But I do have a lot of challenges. Mark and I are always setting goals that challenge us. We always say, "The purpose of setting a really big goal is not so that you can achieve it so much, but it's who you become in the process of achieving it." A friend of mine, Jim Rohn, says, "You want to set goals big enough so that in the process of achieving them you become someone worth being."

I think that to be a millionaire is nice but so what? People make the money and then they lose it. People get the big houses and then they burn down or Silicon Valley goes belly up and all of a sudden they don't have a big house anymore. But who you became in the process of learning how to be successful can never be taken away from you. So what we do is constantly put big challenges in front of us.

We have a book called *Chicken Soup for the Teacher's Soul*. (You'll have to make sure to get a copy for your wife.) I was a teacher and a teacher trainer for years. But because of the success of the *Chicken Soup* books I haven't been in the education world that much. I've got to go out and relearn how I market to that world. I met with a Superintendent of Schools. I met with a guy named Jason Dorsey who's one of the number one consultants in the world in that area. I found out who has the bestselling book in that area. I sat down with his wife for a day and talked about her marketing approaches.

I believe that if you face any kind of adversity, whether it's losing your job, your spouse dies, you get divorced, you're in an accident like Christopher Reeve and become paralyzed, or whatever, you simply do what you have to do. You find out who's already handled the problem and how did they've handled it. Then you get the support you need to get through it by their example. Whether it's a counselor in your church or you go on a retreat or you read the Bible, you do something that gives you the support you need to get to the other end.

You also have to know what the end is that you want to have. Do you want to be remarried? Do you just want to have a job and be a single mom? What is it? If you reach out and ask for support I think you'll get help. People really like to help other people. They're not always available because sometimes they're going through problems also; but there's always someone with a helping hand.

Often I think we let our pride get in the way. We let our stubbornness get in the way. We let our belief in how the world should be interfere and get in our way instead of dealing with how the world is. When we get that out of that way then we can start doing that which we need to do to get where we need to go.

WRIGHT

If you could have a platform and tell our audience something you feel that would help or encourage them, what would you say?

CANFIELD

I'd say number one is to believe in yourself, believe in your dreams, and trust your feelings. I think too many people are trained wrong when they're little kids. For example, when kids are mad at their daddy they're told, "You're not mad at your Daddy."

They say, "Gee, I thought I was."

Or the kid says, "That's going to hurt," and the doctor says, "No it's not." Then they give you the shot and it hurts. They say, "See that didn't hurt, did it?" When that happened to you as a kid, you started to not trust yourself.

You may have asked your mom, "Are you upset?" and she says, "No," but she really was. So you stop learning to trust your perception.

I tell this story over and over. There are hundreds of people I've met who've come from upper class families where they make big incomes and the dad's a doctor. The kid wants to be a mechanic and work in an auto shop because that's what he loves. The family says, "That's beneath us. You can't do that." So the kid ends up being an anesthesiologist killing three people because he's not paying attention. What he really wants to do is tinker with cars.

I tell people you've got to trust your own feelings, your own motivations, what turns you on, what you want to do, what makes you feel good, and quit worrying about what other people say, think, and want for you. Decide what you want for yourself and then do what you need to do to go about getting it. It takes work.

I read a book a week minimum and at the end of the year I've read fifty-two books. We're talking about professional books—books on self-help, finances, psychology, parenting, and so forth. At the end of ten years I've read 520 books. That puts me in the top 1 percent of people knowing important information in this country. But most people are spending their time watching television.

When I went to work for W. Clement Stone, he told me, "I want you to cut out one hour a day of television."

"Okay," I said, "what do I do with it?"

"Read," he said.

He told me what kind of books to read. He said, "At the end of a year you'll have spent 365 hours reading. Divide that by a forty-hour work week and that's nine and a half weeks of education every year."

I thought, "Wow, that's two months." It was like going back to summer school.

As a result of his advice I have close to 8,000 books in my library. The reason I'm involved in this book project instead of someone else is that people like me, Jim Rohn, Les Brown, and you read a lot. We listen to tapes and we go to seminars. That's why we're the people with the information.

I always say that your raise becomes effective when you do. You'll become more effective as you gain more skills, more insight, and more knowledge.

WRIGHT

Jack, I have watched your career for a long time and your accomplishments are just outstanding. But your humanitarian efforts are really what impress me. I think that you're doing great things not only in California, but all over the country.

CANFIELD

It's true. In addition to all of the work we do, we pick one to three charities and we've given away over six million dollars in the last eight years, along with our publisher who matches every penny we give away. We've planted over a million trees in Yosemite National Park. We've bought hundreds of thousands of cataract operations in third world countries. We've contributed to the Red Cross, the Humane Society, and on it goes. It feels like a real blessing to be able to make that kind of a contribution to the world.

WRIGHT

Today we have been talking with Jack Canfield, founder and co-creator of the *Chicken Soup for the Soul* book series. Chicken Soup for the Soul reaches people well beyond the bookstore, with CD and DVD collections, company-sponsored samplers, greeting cards, children's entertainment products, pet food, flowers, and many other products in line with Chicken Soup for the Soul's purpose. Chicken Soup for the Soul is currently implementing a plan to expand into all media by working with television networks on several shows and developing a major Internet presence dedicated to life improvement, emotional support, and inspiration.

CANFIELD

Another book I've written is *The Success Principles*. In it I share sixty-four principles that other people and I have utilized to achieve great levels of success.

WRIGHT

I will stand in line to get one of those. Thank you so much being with us.

JACK CANFIELD is one of America's leading experts on developing self-esteem and peak performance. A dynamic and entertaining speaker, as well as a highly sought-after trainer, he has a wonderful ability to inform and inspire audiences toward developing their own human potential and personal effectiveness.

Jack Canfield is most well-known for the *Chicken Soup for the Soul* series, which he co-authored with Mark Victor Hansen, and for his audio programs about building high self-esteem. Jack is the founder of Self-Esteem Seminars, located in Santa Barbara, California, which trains entrepreneurs, educators, corporate leaders, and employees how to accelerate the achievement of their personal and professional goals. Jack is also founder of The Foundation for Self Esteem, located in Culver City, California, which provides self-esteem resources and training to social workers, welfare recipients, and human resource professionals.

Jack graduated from Harvard in 1966, received his ME degree at the University of Massachusetts in 1973, and earned an Honorary Doctorate from the University of Santa Monica. He has been a high school and university teacher, a workshop facilitator, a psychotherapist, and a leading authority in the area of self-esteem and personal development.

As a result of his work with prisoners, welfare recipients, and inner-city youth, Jack was appointed by the State Legislature to the California Task Force to Promote Self-Esteem and Personal and Social Responsibility. He also served on the Board of Trustees of the National Council for Self-Esteem.

JACK CANFIELD
The Jack Canfield Companies
P.O. Box 30880
Santa Barbara, CA 93130
Phone: 805.563.2935
Fax: 805.563.2945
www.jackcanfield.com

CHAPTER THREE

Stepping Stones to an Inspired Life

DAVID WRIGHT (WRIGHT)

Today we're talking with Samy Chong. As a young boy, Samy dreamed of owning his own business. After putting himself through university, he fulfilled his dream and became a wildly successful restaurateur and caterer. But for Samy, that wasn't enough. After reading a letter from his daughter in 2001 that questioned why he wasn't following his passion and making a difference in the world, he had an awakening. This was the turning point that led him to pursue his calling. Since becoming a certified coach in 2005, his practice continues to thrive and he remains passionate about serving today's business leaders by helping them make positive, sustainable changes.

Samy, welcome to *Stepping Stones to Success*.

SAMY CHONG (CHONG)

Thank you, David. It's an honor and a pleasure to be here.

WRIGHT

So what made you want to have your own business at such a young age?

CHONG

At fourteen, I had a dream while working as a dishwasher in a restaurant. From that dream I just knew that one day I would have a restaurant with white tablecloths, candles on each table, and beautiful music would be playing in the background. Sure enough, that dream came true when I was twenty-five. I now know, without a doubt, it happened because I really, really wanted it and believed it would happen. When a dream is sealed by a sense of purpose, unyielding passion, and a desire to serve, it's bound to come true. I believe this is why the restaurant became a reality for me.

WRIGHT

How did you make the transition from restaurateur to executive coach? What steps were involved?

CHONG

It began in March 2001 while I was on vacation in New York City with my two children. For some reason, when we returned home to Toronto, the kids shared that on this trip I hadn't been their usual fun-loving father. The typical "off-the-wall" dynamic we had was absent. To them I was stressed and "off."

When we arrived home I left them at my place while I went to check in on my restaurant. I then drove them back to their mother's home—my wonderful former wife, who lives a couple of hours away. By the time I returned home it was after midnight.

I was looking forward to getting a good sleep so I got undressed and then turned the bed covers over to crawl in. I immediately noticed a letter that had been placed between the sheets written by my thirteen-year-old daughter. It was four and a half pages long. In it, she wrote: "Dad, what are you doing? You love to help people. You love to live a passionate life. You have a spiritual side you love to talk about. What are you doing?" My son, who was nine at the time, had cut out pieces of paper that said "I love you" and hid them everywhere. It turns out these two kids had been busy trying to care for their father while I was away taking care of the restaurant.

That night, after reading the letter over and over, I had a complete meltdown. I cried uncontrollably and as I did, the realization came to me that I was staying in the restaurant business because of the money. This was the only experience I'd had. It was all I knew how to do and over the years it had provided a good lifestyle for my family and me. It became clear to me that as much as I loved it, it was no longer the way for me to honor who I was. So I put the restaurant up for sale not knowing what I was going to do next. My accountant, who had been doing my books for eighteen years, knew the kind of sales we did and decided he would buy it outright.

It's interesting to note that in the year after I sold the restaurant 9/11 occurred and here in Toronto, Canada, we had an outbreak of severe acute respiratory syndrome (SARS), a pneumonia-like disease. Then a case of mad cow disease in Western Canada hit the news, followed by another episode of SARS. These events collectively devastated much of the restaurant industry in our city. In hindsight it was clear that I had sold the restaurant at the height of the market just before the value of the restaurant would have dropped significantly due to circumstances beyond my control.

Then the question arose as to what was I going to do next? I had no idea or direction, therefore I took a month off and traveled with a friend to Greece. After the break I returned home and within weeks someone suggested I take a coaching course from The Coaches Training Institute (CTI).

The minute I went to that first class I knew that this was my calling. The experience was a crucial lesson for me in learning to surrender. I can best summarize it by taking a quote from Joseph Campbell's book, *The Myth*, "When you follow your bliss ... doors will open where you would not have thought there would be doors; and where there wouldn't be a door for anyone else." That is how I transitioned from my life as a restaurant owner to life as an executive coach.

I like to think that for the first forty years of my life I served and nourished the human body and for the next forty plus years I'm going to serve and nourish the mind, soul, and spirit.

WRIGHT

So what do you love about pursuing your passion—coaching?

CHONG

When I look around our world today there is just simply too much pain and suffering. There are too many people struggling, not realizing that the life they have chosen was never meant to be difficult. It's only difficult when we're not honoring our purpose on this Earth. It's challenging sometimes because we're not following what I call the law of the spirit—the natural law. Or we're choosing thoughts that allow us to continually attract what we don't want.

Part of the reason I'm so passionate about this calling is because the more we're able to help people raise their consciousness and awareness, the greater happiness and fulfillment they'll find in all facets of their life. As a coach I get a chance to help people make significant changes in their life, which in turn fulfills my passion and allows me to live my purpose. The rewards are in the positive results I see and hear from my clients and their circles of influence.

WRIGHT

So who inspires you?

CHONG

I have a number of sources of inspiration. The earliest one I can remember, from my late teens, was Dr. Wayne Dyer who touched me through his books and tapes. I love his work. Over the years, as he continues to grow and evolve, I better understand his core messages of self-empowerment, contentment, and spacious serenity. To this day I read each new book he writes, follow his teachings, and appreciate the guidance his wisdom gives me.

Another source of inspiration was my father. He was a very successful mining executive in Malaysia before he and my mother decided to join their children (my three siblings and me) who had already immigrated to Canada. My father arrived here in his early fifties and the only job he could find, because of the language barrier, was stuffing foam into furniture in a factory. The back of his hands and his knuckles were always either bleeding or cracked from the beating they took daily. I remember making a vow to myself that one day I would have a business of my own where my father could come and go as he wished. He could take as much money as he wanted because I was going to take care of him. That heartfelt desire helped give me the inspiration to keep moving toward my dream.

My children continue to be a huge source of inspiration to me. What makes them so special, aside from the letter and love notes that I mentioned earlier, is that they are my teachers. I learned from them, even while they were toddlers, that anything was possible. It was refreshing to watch them at a stage when there was no concept of limitations. My kids inspire me today, as young adults, with their amazing energy and spirit. It's wonderful to be able to stay open and learn from them as much as they're able to learn from me.

Another significant source of inspiration in my life is the library. At any time, whatever I'm feeling, I know that a visit to the library will allow me to touch so many intimate experiences through the written word. I am filled by the richness of authors' wisdom and experience. It is a never-ending resource for expanding my knowledge and understanding of all things.

My connection with my divine source is a daily inspiration. I believe that my quiet time—those magical moments every morning when I spend time contemplating or meditating—allows me to think from a very different perspective. It never fails to set a positive tone for the rest of my day.

Lastly, there's something about nature that destresses me—like pushing my reset button—whether it's hiking in the woods or sitting by water. Nature has a way of rejuvenating the soul and cleansing the mind of worries.

The above are my key sources of inspiration, which collectively contribute to allowing me to live the kind of life that has and continues to awaken me to all that life offers.

WRIGHT

The title of our book is *Stepping Stones to Success*. How do you define success?

CHONG

I really love the book title because a few years ago I partnered with a fellow coach to lead a tele-class series called "Stepping Stones to Inner Peace." So when you invited me to be part of this book project, it resonated deeply with me.

The way I define success is by establishing how much inner peace and contentment a person has. For me, if your success is measured by the external recognition of a title or the kind of car you drive or your status in the community, then I can pretty much guarantee that your source of joy and contentment will never be sustainable. Therefore, success is what I refer to as an "inside job."

During the last holiday season prior to the sale of the restaurant, when we had had yet another set of record-breaking results, a customer came up to me and said, "Samy, you must be really, really happy that the restaurant is doing so well." I don't know what prompted me, but I replied, "If I'm happy because the restaurant business is good, then in mid-February when we may have a huge snowstorm and only do two or three tables, I must be one very unhappy restaurateur." My point is that if my joy and happiness is dictated by the external environment, then I know it is not sustainable.

Part of my definition of success is an inner contentment and peace. It's like living a life without struggle and knowing that everything is okay the way it is. My joy and happiness is independent of the outer circumstances. A clue that I am on the right path is that synchronicity and coincidence occur more frequently in my life. It is like I'm living in the moment yet aware of where I'm going and what I wish to experience.

A restaurant is what I always wanted and when I sold my first one I knew there was going to be another more upscale restaurant I would find to purchase. I had used the proceeds of the sale of my first restaurant to purchase an investment property, therefore I was at a loss as to where the money would come from when I found my next restaurant. The question was answered a few years later when I bought one that was going through a bankruptcy proceeding. When I was ready to sell this second restaurant I also *knew* the price that I wanted. My accountant knew its true worth and bought it. There have been many significant moments in my life when I just *knew* what I wanted and did not deviate from that belief. That knowingness allows me to continuously attract all that I desire to experience in this wonderful life.

Part of sharing these very personal experiences of success with our readers is to define the difference between a belief and knowing. *Knowing* is a more powerful emotion than believing. When you begin to *know* what is or will happen and when you are not attached to when or how it will happen, something shifts inside you. It's like all your worries and fears dissipate because of your *knowingness*. There's a greater sense of faith and trust *within* that you start to develop. I began to develop my knowingness years ago, so it is now part of my core being. The significant milestones in my life are all marked by this internal knowledge. There is no option other than my intention being fulfilled because of my *knowingness*.

This is best expressed in the biblical verse from Matthew 6:33, "But seek first his kingdom and his righteousness, and all these things will be given to you as well." That's a great summary of how I define success.

WRIGHT

So what would be the stepping stones for you to share with others on how to achieve sustainable success?

CHONG

In the following I will share what I use as the foundation of my personal coaching practice. The four pillars that sustain this success journey are: Purpose, Pain, Passion, and Priorities. I believe that every one of us comes to this Earth for a specific experience and that experience is as unique as our thumbprint. With close to seven billion people on this planet, that accounts for a mind-boggling number of unique prints. This means every one of our experiences — what I call purpose — is very different. So the first stone is to learn and understand what our purpose is — what are we doing here and what's the significant highlight or learning of our time here? Once we become more aware of our learning, we will begin to live a purpose-filled life.

The second stone is pain. Each of us has unfinished business from our past experiences that we need to deal with. If we haven't processed our past pain — whether it be from a failed business or partnership or somebody betraying us deeply or finding ourselves disconnected from the people we love — whatever the pain is, it keeps us from moving forward.

As of this writing I'm in the midst of a new relationship after fifteen years of being on my own after my marriage ended. I realize that my heart is still protected because of the hurt I felt at the time of my divorce. Until I learn to release that pain, it will have an affect on my current relationship in terms of my ability to be intimate and to trust. So there's something about pain in the past that needs to be released in order to be resolved in our hearts. Otherwise it will always get in the way of our current and future successes.

Next is passion. Each of us in our heart of hearts has a strong desire that is anchored in passion. Some of us live it well, some of us are barely living it, and still others have buried that passion so deeply they don't even know what it is anymore. Until we rekindle and stir that passion in our core, the meaning and flavor of life is weakened and lacks energy. Living our life with zest and passion fuels our energy and vitality. Passion allows us to move toward our destiny. It is a key ingredient to our lives and sustains all the good things that are happening.

Lastly, we have lots of different priorities that we need to sort out. I subscribe to a television network that has nine hundred and ninety-nine channels. If I were to surf from channel one to nine hundred and ninety-nine, it would take me just under forty-five minutes. I have now programmed the important channels so that when I do one cycle of surfing it takes seven to eight minutes. This is just one example of the many distractions that we have in our lives. Most of us now have a handheld device strapped to our hip or in our purse and at any given moment we can be interrupted by an e-mail, phone call, text message, or voice mail. We are kept busy by all of these distractions. No wonder many of us feel a sense of attention deficit disorder. How can we avoid it when we don't know our priorities? As humans we do not have enough random access memory (RAM) in our psyche to contain all this stimuli. No wonder we often feel like we're breaking apart when we're being tugged in so many directions.

These four stepping stones — Purpose, Pain, Passion, and Priorities — are critical to our continuous progress and well-being. If we wish to achieve all that we desire and deserve, we must step on each of these stones.

WRIGHT

So what steps would you recommend to people looking to pursue their purpose and passion?

CHONG

From my own experience, the first step is to uncover what your purpose and passion is so you can clarify what you want to experience in your life. Then quantify it and make sure you're able to visualize it with all your emotional energy. It is like living that perfect experience in your mind.

Second, learn to surrender and know that what you really, really want is coming. Release the will to know when and how things will happen. Know that this invisible intelligence that I choose to call God will make it happen. After all, worries and anxieties are a method of praying for what you don't want. They actually serve to slow down the process.

The third step is to imagine three intertwined circles. Circle one is what you would do if money, your mortgage, and any other financial responsibilities were no longer issues for you. What would you do every day? Where would you go? What would inspire you to get out of bed every morning enthusiastically embracing the day ahead?

Circle two is identifying the greatest need in our world today—what are we all seeking and what would allow our world to have greater peace and contentment?

Circle three identifies the resources required to support these thoughts and ideas. Your vocation can be found in the area where the three circles overlap.

The fourth step for people who are looking to pursue their purpose and passion is through sharing with a group of like-minded people who meet regularly, such as a mastermind group or through having a coach in your life to help you navigate the path.

WRIGHT

What are the most important lessons you've learned so far in your life around success?

CHONG

For me, there are five key lessons that I believe are universal. I've learned them and live by them as a result of living a purposeful life. I do the things that I love and love what I do. The more grateful I am for this success and abundance, the more I attract the kind of people, energy, and projects I want into my life.

Having the kind of love and relationships around me that support what I do is definitely a bonus.

The first lesson, and this is very important to me, is learning how to *serve*. Part of the reason the restaurant was so incredibly successful was the whole team, from the managers to the dishwashers, understood that we were there for one common purpose—to serve and honor each and every one of our guests as though they were in our homes.

For example, if you came into the restaurant and let us know your birthday, thereafter, every year, we would send you a gift certificate to eat anything in the restaurant for free without any preconditions. Now imagine people coming in saying to us, "You mean I don't have to bring anybody?" Nope. "You mean it's not like I buy one and get one free or 50 percent off?" Nope. "You mean I can order anything I want?" Absolutely yes! We would have on our menu the most delicious range of entrees that we would serve for free. That was the kind of hospitality we were known for. I am certain it contributed to our success.

I remember another story from my restaurant days that also illustrates the concept of *serving*. A customer came in and asked for a pint of Guinness. We were a fine dining restaurant with an extensive wine selection, but we did *not* serve draft beer. So imagine me carrying a pint of Guinness in the middle of Toronto from the nearest pub down the street to this guest! The kind of publicity that we received from this man was incredible. Everywhere he went he recounted the story of how special he felt as a guest of our restaurant. Without reservation we understood the meaning of hospitality, of opening our hearts and arms, and having others do so in return. So for me the lesson is honoring the art of servitude and always caring about people.

The second lesson is to simply never stop learning. I believe that learning fuels our minds just as nourishment fuels our bodies. The more we're able to learn, unlearn, and relearn, the more we're able to find different ways to serve, to live on purpose, and to do the kinds of things we want. Learning really allows us to continue to stretch, grow, and evolve.

The third lesson is to be mindful of all your thoughts. After all, your dominant thoughts always become your reality. What you think about becomes your truth. Therefore, worry and negative thoughts have energy that move you toward the very experiences that you do *not* want to create. We all have brilliant minds, but most of the time our minds run our lives rather than the other way around.

For example, when you cannot sleep at night, your mind has one thought and then another, then another, then, when we finish the last thought, we start from the top all over again. That's how our mind can run us and, in effect, run our lives. When we begin to have what I call a greater mindfulness or consciousness, we start to choose thoughts that we want to think, versus our minds choosing the thoughts for us to think. That's why I embrace the first habit, in Stephen Covey's, *The 7 Habits of Highly Effective People.* He states that "between stimulus and response, between what happened to us and how we respond, there is a gap. The bigger we can make that gap, the better chance we have to choose a response instead of a reaction." By being mindful of this habit we will continue to grow and evolve.

Over time we will begin to cultivate what I call a "witness within you." It's as though you become the observer of your life. The more we are able to watch ourselves and yet be fully engaged, the more we're practicing living *in* this world, but not *of* this world. We're all spiritual beings having a human experience, rather than human beings having a spiritual experience. From this higher perspective we are able to become more conscious.

The fourth lesson is being in gratitude for all that you have and all that you are experiencing. The law of attraction states that the more you are in gratitude of what you have and love, the more you will be given the very things that you desire. This is a simple law and yet many of us fail to acknowledge what we have. We forget when enough is enough. A good daily reminder is to say, as you get out of bed in the morning, "Thank," when you put your first foot on the floor, and when your second foot touches the floor say, "You." It is a powerful affirmation of gratitude that truly starts your day off on the right foot. (Pardon the pun.)

The last lesson is to deal with every one of your fears at this moment. Fear has a way of attracting more of those fear-based experiences in your life. It's as though you can never get enough of what you *don't* want or are fearful of—a powerful attractor until you neutralize it.

These lessons are tools that serve as reminders to me of how far I have come and how joyful it is to continue on this evolving journey called life.

WRIGHT

So what are you working on now?

CHONG

I'm writing a book dealing with the subject of death. It's a difficult subject for most, as we often struggle with how to talk about, let alone embrace it, yet we are all aware of the affect it has on us. I have this simple premise that if we don't know how to die, how do we know how to live? Most of our lives are spent planning for our future but little time is spent planning for our death. Death is certain and life is uncertain. Once we have a better understanding of death we may choose to live a very different life. The two go hand in hand.

This book is the next step forward for me in continuing to uncover my purpose and passion. My desire is that this most fearful subject need not have such a hold on us. If we're able to know how to handle and deal with this ultimate fear, then there's nothing to stop us from creating whatever we want in our lives — or in this world.

WRIGHT

Why is this book important to you?

CHONG

I believe that my book will provide answers to some sought-after questions. The youngest Baby Boomers are now turning fifty. We're becoming more aware of our mortality en masse. We potentially have fewer days left here on Earth than we've already lived. That is a sobering thought. We have parents or grandparents who are facing their deaths and many of us find it hard to navigate through this process of saying goodbye. A lot of the time our pain and grief only happens after they are gone because of unfinished business between us.

I now know that a lot of this can be avoided if we begin to understand how to have conversations on the subject of death. My intention is that the book will provide the wisdom and skills to help guide us through the discomfort that death brings to the surface. In all the literature I've read that deals with the subject of death, I discovered that you cannot deal with death without dealing with life, nor can you deal with life without dealing with death.

Collectively, we're at a place in human evolution where a lot of us have had many experiences — both positive and negative. We've accomplished a lot and now we're beginning to wonder what's next. We're questioning the meaning behind being here on Earth. For me there's something about this book that allows people to really examine their life and to have a firmer grip and understanding of life and its meaning. It's really about continuously dealing with unfinished business so that we all may live and die without regrets.

If something happened to me tomorrow (God forbid), have I done what I need to do and said what I needed to say? It's interesting to note that my friends always say I'm by far the most positive and optimistic person they know. And yet, it's asking this seemingly negative question that allows me to live my life more fully. It helps me *not* take a single day for granted. Living with this kind of heightened awareness allows me to always stay in the moment.

WRIGHT

So looking ahead where do you see yourself in ten years?

CHONG

I see myself using all these core principles to help raise the consciousness of mankind on a grander scale. Again, it comes back to my core belief that life is meant to be easy. Pain may be necessary but suffering is definitely optional. As the Baby Boomers move toward the last chapter of their lives they are seeking a sense of contentment blended with joyfulness and genuine heartfelt fulfillment. I will continue to speak about the perspective I'm sharing with you here today. I will write more books and coach more people forward. On a personal note, I'll continue to learn to surrender and totally live the divine will of what I came to this Earth to do.

WRIGHT

So what will sustain that success mentality?

CHONG

The kinds of concepts, beliefs, and knowingness that we've talked about will sustain the success mentality. There is a Margaret Young quote that summarizes it best: "Often people attempt to live their lives backward; they try to have more things, or more money, in order to do more of what they want, so they will be happier. The way it actually works is the reverse. You must first be who you really are, then do what you need to do, in order to have what you want."

WRIGHT

Well, what a great conversation. I've learned a lot here today, especially the Purpose, Pain, Passion, and Priorities. I really appreciate all the time you've spent with me and I believe yours is a message that will be well received by our readers.

CHONG

Thank you, David. I have enjoyed connecting with you. I am hopeful that the messages contained in this chapter as well as the insight I'll be providing through my book on death will be embraced by your readers.

WRIGHT

Today we've been talking with Samy Chong. Since becoming a Certified Coach in 2005 and achieving his Master Certified Coach (MCC) designation in

2009, he remains passionate about serving today's business leaders by coaching them to make positive and sustainable changes.

Samy, thank you so much for being with us today on *Stepping Stones to Success.*

CHONG

And, Mr. David Wright, I'm grateful for what you're doing as a publisher. Thanks for being part of this *Stepping Stones to Success* interview.

SAMY CHONG is an executive coach, inspirational speaker, and Chief Inspirational Officer (CIO) of Corporate Philosopher Inc.. Samy coaches senior leaders who have exhausted traditional methods of solving challenges and who seek inspiration and direction by aligning their passion and life purpose. Through his work, Samy honors his core values of integrity and living life to the fullest, sharing his unique ideas about spirituality in business and his passion for inspiring others to greatness.

SAMY CHONG CPCC MCC
302-14 Deer Park Crescent
Toronto, Ontario
Canada M4V 2C2
(416) 347-2814
CorporatePhilosopher-SamyChong@Rogers.com
www.corporatephilosopher.com

CHAPTER FOUR

The Ultimate Success: Living a Happy Life

DAVID WRIGHT (WRIGHT)

Today we are talking with David Humes, CHt. David is a happiness coach and workshop facilitator. He is a Certified Hypnotherapist, a Certified NLP Practitioner, a professional member of the National Speakers Association, an ordained minister, and an internationally certified second degree black belt in Wado-Ryu karate. He has presented over eight hundred full day seminars to thousands of attendees in forty-eight states and throughout Canada for clients that include Verizon, DirecTV, Johns Hopkins University, ITT Technical Institute, and many others.

David, welcome to *Stepping Stones to Success.*

How do you define success?

DAVID HUMES, CHt (HUMES)

In my opinion, the ultimate success is living a happy life.

WRIGHT

How do you define living a happy life?

HUMES

Everyone has his or her own definition of happiness. However, if you want to live a happy life, then you may want to model people who are living a happy life and adopt their definition, which includes the following:

- Wanting what you have; being grateful for things and appreciative of the people in your life
- Having loving personal relationships; having a support group
- Doing what you love for a living in environmentally responsible service to others
- Living in the present moment, which means being fully engaged in what you're doing and not being tormented by the past or anxious about the future
- A deep sense of wellbeing that comes from knowing you can handle whatever life brings to you
- Being in truth with yourself and living *your* values, not someone else's.

WRIGHT

What's the fastest way to succeed at being happy now?

HUMES

Make a list of what you are grateful for. Read your list and try to get the feeling of gratitude as soon as you wake up every morning and in the evening right before you go to bed. If you only do this once a day, do it in the morning.

I actually made a recording of what I'm grateful for and instead of a loud, obnoxious alarm clock that startles me out of my sleep, I'm gently awakened with the cassette tape that plays my voice reminding me of what I'm grateful for. It's a great way to begin your day. Rather than focusing on what you *don't* have, this helps you focus on, and be thankful for, what you *do* have.

Here's something else you can do right now. Imagine that you're on a business trip alone, in another country. As far as you know, everything is okay back home with your family.

When your plane arrives nine hours later, you notice on the television, as you're walking through the airport, that there was a fire in what looks like your neighborhood. You stop to watch and notice what looks like your house being burned to the ground.

Your cell phone battery is dead, so you begin frantically looking for a public telephone. Notice how you're feeling right now. What are you thinking about?

You finally get in touch with your significant other who tells you that everyone is okay. The house and everything in it was totally destroyed, but everyone survived, even the dog and the cat.

Now how do you feel about the situation? Think about it for a moment. Most people could care less about the house and would feel eternally grateful that everyone was alive and okay. Things can be replaced; your loved ones can't.

This is the feeling you need to remember when small things, insignificant things, non-essential, or even "big" things bother you. Remind yourself of these grateful feelings you have toward your loved ones first thing every morning and every evening as you drift off to sleep. It's impossible to be grateful and unhappy at the same time.

WRIGHT

If I'm happy now, won't that diminish my motivation to succeed on a higher level?

HUMES

Actually, the studies show the opposite to be true.

When you're not happy or when you're not happily achieving your goals, you tend to experience more stress, frustration, and anger along the way. These negative emotions in your body actually contribute to disease. You'll notice it in the weakest part of your body first. So how can having a weakened immune system and poor health add to your motivation to achieve your goals? It can't.

When you're happy or when you happily achieve, you experience positive emotions such as compassion, gratitude, and joy. These positive emotions release powerful chemicals that support great health in your body. This has now been scientifically proven.

So, given the choice — and you *do* have a choice — which decision do you think will diminish your motivation to succeed more: happily achieving your goals in good health or unhappily struggling to achieve your goals in a body that is steadily declining in health?

When you're happy, you experience less stress. When you experience less stress, you're able to do more productive work, better quality work, and with less errors. When you happily achieve, it's the negative spiral in reverse. I call it the positive spiral to health, wealth, happiness, and the abundance of all good things. Success begets more success. Happiness begets more happiness.

If you want more "stuff" because you think it will make you happy, it won't. Study after study shows that more "stuff" or more money does not make you significantly happier in the long run. The only exception to this is if you are below the poverty level. Then, once you rise above poverty, more money or success doesn't make you significantly happier in the long run.

When you achieve a goal, you may experience a spurt of short-term happiness, and that's okay. But it doesn't last long. You need to get another "fix" in order to feel happy or successful.

That's the trap a lot of people fall into: the philosophy of "more." "When I get this new house, then I will be happy. When I get this new car, then I will be happy. When I get out of debt, then I will be happy." Then you get the new house and new car and out of debt and you say, "When I get this *bigger* house or *another* house, *then* I will be happy" and so on. It never ends. You can never be satisfied or happy *unless* you change your *definition* of success to "living a happy life," rather than the philosophy of "more, more, more."

I don't have a problem with having goals or being ambitious. You should have a direction in your life. A personal purpose statement and goals give you that. But if you want to be happy *now* and in the future, regardless of what happens, don't *condition* your happiness on the achievement of your goals. Choose to be happy now and then happily achieve.

People like to be around happy people and don't like to be around unhappy people. Interestingly, when you're happy you attract more happiness and success.

WRIGHT

What do you think are the biggest obstacles people face in trying to become successful at living a happy life?

HUMES

The only obstacle that we ever have is our thinking. We all see the world through our own unique perspective, belief filter, or Belief System (I call it "BS" for short).

Our BS has been determined and influenced by the choices we've made about our upbringing, the television shows we watch, radio programs and/or audio recordings we listen to, the books we read, the people we associate with, what we say to ourselves, and how we re-present our experiences in our mind with pictures, sounds, and feelings.

The good news is that we can change our BS. Knowing this should give us hope. We are the ultimate deciders of our BS.

If you have a worthwhile goal and at the same time you believe that you don't deserve it or that it's not possible, chances are extremely good that you won't achieve it. If you do achieve it, you'll probably sabotage your success to come back in line with your self-perception, your self-image, or what you believe (BS) you deserve or is possible.

So believing that you don't deserve success is one obstacle for some people to overcome. Not believing that success is possible for you is another. Two more common beliefs you must get rid of, if you have them, are the fear of success and the fear of failure.

The fear of success causes you to do things, mostly unconsciously, to guarantee that you will only succeed at a certain level. It's as though you have your success thermostat set to "mediocrity."

The fear of failure may stop you from even trying, because you link too much pain to failing.

Thinking that you have to be a certain age, a certain weight, a certain height, a certain race, or look a certain way are all self-imposed limitations that we create in our mind. All of these (BS) beliefs are in essence saying, "When I'm the perfect age (or weight, or height, or race, or look a certain way), then I'll be successful." If you have to wait for these things to happen in order for you to be successful, aren't you living in the future or waiting for, as Dr. Denis Waitley so eloquently put it, "Someday Isle"?

Remember, there is no past—it is dust, concrete, and can't be changed. There is no future—it has yet to manifest. There is only the eternal *now*. Extremely happy people know that it is vitally important to live consciously in the present moment.

Another huge obstacle to living a happy life is what I call "conditional happiness" and having the philosophy of "more," as I mentioned above. "When I have more time, then I will be happy or successful." Or, "When I have more money, then I will be happy or successful." Or, "When I have more friends, then I will be happy or successful." Or, "When I have more cars, then I will be happy or successful." Or, "When I have more homes, then I will be happy or successful." Or, "When I have more toys (big screen televisions, iPhones, Xbox, etc.), then I will be happy or successful."

Forget all of that and simply choose to be happy now—unconditionally. When you feel that you deserve to be happy now for no reason, it's easy. (Read "Unconditional Happiness" on Happy23-7.com).

WRIGHT

What's the formula for living a happy life?

HUMES

Decide to be happy. Make it your intention to be happy with everything you do. When you start with a strong intention (choice) to be happy, you will attract the "how-to." The happiness decision needs to be made in the present moment on an ongoing basis. Every time something comes up that challenges your happiness, you get another opportunity make the choice to be happy or unhappy. If there is something you're doing or that comes up that makes you unhappy, delegate it, avoid it if possible, or stop doing it all together. It's your choice.

Take responsibility for your happiness. Playing the victim, which is a Belief System (BS), takes away your power. Even if you are truly being "victimized," happy, responsible people look for what's good about the situation or what *could be* good about it. Be optimistic. Look for the life lesson in every situation. When you believe that you have some control in your life, you will be happier and healthier. Beliefs are made up and ultimately determined by you. Ask, "Does this belief contribute to my happiness or not?"

Taking responsibility for your happiness includes taking responsibility for your mental and emotional health. There is a lot you can do on your own in terms of self-help/self-therapy, but if you need professional help, by all means get it. Anti-depressant drugs may be prescribed in severe cases by psychiatrists, but they are meant to be a short-term solution and come with lots of negative side effects, including making it harder to live in the present moment. Cognitive therapy and mindfulness meditation are excellent tools for mastering your thoughts and emotions, reducing stress, and learning how to live more consistently in the present moment, all extremely helpful for living a happy life.

Make a list of what you love doing. Schedule these things in your calendar so you'll actually do them.

Do what you love for a living in environmentally responsible service to others, and if you *can't yet* do what you love for a living, do what you love as a *hobby* until you *can* do it for a living.

Develop and maintain loving personal relationships. Schedule time daily, weekly, or monthly to keep in contact with your core support groups—family, friends, church, hobby, or club members. Don't forget the most important relationship you'll ever have is *with yourself!* Love and accept yourself unconditionally. Then you can be more empathetic and compassionate toward others.

Feel gratitude for what you have and appreciate the people in your life. Remind yourself of the things for which you are grateful the first thing every morning. If you appreciate someone, tell him or her. Start a gratitude journal. Write in it every day or at least once a week. Review it regularly.

Commit to lifelong learning. Recent studies have shown that people who perennially read, do crossword puzzles, or otherwise learn new things reduce the onset of Alzheimer's disease and slow down the aging process. It increases neuroplasticity, creating new neurological pathways, which keeps your mind sharp.

Clarify your purpose and values — not someone else's values, *your* values. Strive to live your values. Live the truth of who you are.

Learn from the past, plan for the future, and live in the present. To free yourself from the past, forgive yourself and others. Overcome feelings of guilt and shame. Get cognitive therapy if necessary. Create a compelling future (purpose/goals), but don't condition your happiness on the attainment of that future. Happily achieve. Practice mindfulness meditation to help you live more consciously in the present moment. Keep practicing. It gets better.

WRIGHT

What can I do to stay in the present moment more consistently?

HUMES

Most of the happiness data I've studied conclude that living in the present moment is a common trait of extremely happy people.

Think about it — when you dwell on a negative emotion, you're living in the past or future. Take anger, for example. When anger consumes you, you're living in the past. Someone did something or *you* did something that made you mad. When you ruminate about the event in your mind, the anger continues. In order to stay mad, you have to continually think about and dwell on the past event (i.e., living in the past).

Similarly, when you feel shame or guilt, you're living in the past. Not that you shouldn't feel guilt when you do "wrong" or harm to others, but dwelling there forever won't help you be happy. Make a vow to never do it again or do less of it in the future and move on. Keep trying. You and everyone on the planet is a fallible human being. Accept *yourself* unconditionally and continually try to improve your *behavior*.

When you feel anxiety, you're living in the future, worried about what might happen.

I'm not suggesting that you should push your emotions down and try to hide them or never experience them — far from it! Extremely happy people allow themselves to experience their emotions fully in the present moment. It's called being *alive*. It's possible to *feel* intense emotions without doing anything to hurt others or yourself.

What's good about expressing your emotions fully and completely in the present moment is that when you let your emotions out, they don't fester or grow into explosive drama like a pressure cooker. Let them out now. Be present. You'll feel much better being in truth with what is, rather than trying to create an illusion of how you think you should be or how *it* (life) should be. One of my favorite sayings is "It is what it is."

When you allow yourself to totally feel your emotions, they get released from your body quicker, and then you can focus on constructive next steps to getting back to happy, like forgiveness and gratitude.

I'm not suggesting that people who hurt you shouldn't be held accountable. They should. But for your health and happiness' sake, you should totally experience your emotions *and* forgive those you need to forgive and get back to feeling grateful for what you have. This is not easy for many people, but it's possible and necessary if you want to live in the present moment and live a happy life. Forgiveness is the key to freeing yourself from the bondage of the past.

When you live in the present moment, you are totally focused on what you're doing. There's no one to tell you when you're not living in the present moment, but yourself. There are no "presence police."

My music teacher used to tell me there are three things you need to do in order to master anything—practice, practice, practice! It used to make me mad, but he was right. Mostly.

I wrote an article years ago called "Practice Doesn't Make Perfect." In the article I go on to say that if you practice wrong all day long, you will be very good at doing it wrong. So, practice doesn't make perfect—*perfect practice* makes perfect.

Playing the drums at a professional level for over twenty years taught me a lot about living in the present moment. Perfect practice takes intense, focused concentration and attention over a long period of time, especially when you're the drummer.

If you "space out" for a moment or two and lose your awareness of the present moment, the tempo may drift a bit—faster or slower. What's the job of a drummer? To be the rock solid foundation for the band. Who do they blame when the band rushes (speeds up) or drags (slows down)? The drummer. So the pressure is on to be extremely solid and consistent over time.

During the five-year period when I taught private drum lessons, I would have my students practice at painfully slow speeds with a metronome so they would become conscious of their mistakes. Playing at very slow tempos brings to your conscious awareness your imperfections in your playing. It is more difficult because there is more time in between each beat that you have to be aware of. So you can really hear when you're off, even slightly. You can't correct something you're not conscious of.

"If you can't play it slow," I would say, "you can't play it fast." What I meant by that was if you can't play it slow perfectly (or nearly perfectly), then you'll be just as sloppy when you play it fast. A professional musician can tell what's wrong when he or she hears a sloppy performance; even casual listeners will know something's not right, even though they might not be able to put their finger on it.

It drove some of my students mad. But the ones who listened to me and actually practiced as instructed made tremendous progress.

When mastering a musical instrument, it's highly critical that you master living in the present moment, at least for the duration of the music you're performing. If you're playing with a band and you lose awareness of the present moment for too long, you may make a mistake and the other members will let you know about it, especially if it's repeated often.

In everyday life, though, staying present doesn't seem that critical or important. In fact, most people spend the majority of their time in trance, like automatons, doing the same routines day in and day out, missing a great deal of their life because of their unconsciousness.

It does take conscious effort or work initially to live in the present moment. But the effort you put into it will reap many positive benefits, including better mental and physical health and a happier life. Over time it becomes easier and easier until one day you become "unconsciously competent" at living in the present moment consistently.

You have to practice noticing. You have to practice paying attention. Here are some suggestions on how to live more in the present moment.

When you do anything, do it exclusively. Stop multitasking.

When you eat, enjoy and savor each and every bite. Don't eat and read. Don't eat and work at your desk. Don't eat and watch television. Eat slower; it's better for your health anyway. Pay attention to the texture and all of the subtle flavors. Enjoy it! When you eat, only eat. This is eating meditation.

When you exercise, only exercise. Pay attention to your breathing. Feel your entire body. Notice how it feels when sweat runs down your face or your back. Pay attention to how your muscles feel when you're stretching. If your mind takes you into the past or future, notice it, let it go, and come back to focusing on your body. This is normal. Keep practicing. This is exercise meditation.

Whatever you do, do it exclusively. You'll get more done when you focus on one task at a time. You're also more likely to experience "flow." Flow is that state where you get so caught up in the moment of doing something that time seems to fly by. You look up and notice that hours have passed by when you thought it was only minutes.

If you're having trouble staying in the present moment, focus on your breathing. Your breath is always in the present moment. There's no need to take over your breath—just notice it. When your mind wanders and you become aware of it, that's good. Becoming aware that your mind is wandering means that you're conscious of it and *that's* what you want—growing in consciousness and awareness of the present moment. This is an "awareness" or "mindfulness" meditation.

You are *not* your thoughts or your body. You (your awareness/consciousness) are the puppeteer in your life. Your thoughts (ego) and body are the puppets, subject to your control.

Keep coming back to your breathing. Keep practicing. Over time the duration that you can hold your attention on the present moment will increase and you will be more consistently and easily living in the present moment, which contributes to greater levels of happiness. It takes work, but isn't living a happy life worth it even if it takes years to achieve? I believe it is.

You wouldn't run a marathon without working up to it gradually. Don't try to meditate for fifteen minutes or more per day at the beginning. Start with one minute a day or even ten seconds five times a day. The key is to get started and get some momentum going. Gradually increase the amount of time spent in mindfulness meditation until you're meditating fifteen to twenty minutes per day.

I like to begin my day with meditation and feeling grateful. It sets the stage for a wonderful day. String enough wonderful days together and you end up living a happy life.

WRIGHT

How do you know that you're happy?

HUMES

There are two types of happiness referred to in positive psychology—eudemonic happiness and hedonic happiness. What's the difference?

Hedonic happiness comes from pursuing pleasure, enjoyment, and comfort, which, if this is your primary focus, can lead to addictions.

Eudemonic happiness comes from pursuing personal growth, development of your potential, achieving personal excellence, and contributing to the lives of others, which, if this is your primary focus, leads to more life satisfaction.

According to Martin Seligman, arguably the father of positive psychology and the author of *Learned Optimism* and *Authentic Happiness,* "Eudemonic pursuits are significantly correlated with life satisfaction whereas hedonic pursuits are not."

Hedonic pursuits only provide temporary, fleeting satisfaction. If you want long-term life satisfaction, go for eudemonic happiness. But still, the challenge with *knowing* that you're happy is that it's subjective. There are no devices that can empirically say that you're happy or not. We're getting closer, though.

We now have the technology to view changes in brain activity in real time using fMRI (functional Magnetic Resonance Imaging).

Tests involving the brains of monks who have logged over ten thousand hours of meditation were observed while they manifested intense states of joy and compassion. They found that the left frontal lobe of the brain lit up like a Christmas tree, leading researchers to believe that happy states and other emotions can be mapped/observed in the brain. Tests involving people who were depressed indicated that this area of the brain was inactive. Anger shows up in a different place. Much more research needs to be done, but this and other cutting edge technology seems to suggest that we will be able to visually observe happiness in the brain.

Most of us take it for granted when things are going well. We usually don't stop to ask ourselves, "Am I happy?" So, knowing that you're happy isn't always glowingly obvious. Most of us know it when we're *un*-happy, though.

When I was twenty-two years old I got married (eloped) for the wrong reasons. To put it mildly, I was not very happy. We were both very immature. We went to several marriage counselors from varying disciplines, including a Catholic priest who basically told us to go home, make love, and it will all be better in the morning. Not.

I decided to use the "Ben Franklin close" technique to help me make a very important and difficult decision. The "Ben Franklin close" is a sales technique to help prospects make a decision, hopefully to buy the product or service that you're selling. What you do is take out a piece of paper and write down the decision you are considering at the top of the page. Under that you put a line across the top and down the middle of the page and at the top you write "pros" on one side and "cons" on the other and then you list the pros and cons. Next, total up your answers and your answer is made for you. You need to consider the importance or weight of each answer in your final accounting.

What I discovered is that I was 40 percent happy and 60 percent unhappy. I decided to face the truth and answer this very difficult question: "Am I willing to live the rest of my life with a high probability of being only 40 percent happy?"

That was the most difficult question I've ever had to ask myself and answer up until that time. But the answer came. It was a resounding "No!" After I made that decision, I cried for about two hours. I felt like a total failure. But in retrospect, I'm glad that I did it.

If you're considering marriage or an intimate relationship, what I learned from this experience is that if you're less happy *with* someone than you are with*out* them, then you might want to consider looking for another partner. In my opinion, only when being *with* someone makes you a better person or happier than being *without* them, should you continue the relationship.

If you're in a marriage or a committed relationship, especially if you have children, you should exhaust all options in working things out. If you're both committed to making the relationship work, then half of the problem is solved. If this is the case, here's something I learned from Jack Canfield that you can do to improve your relationship:

Ask each other the following questions once a week:

"On a scale of one to ten, how would you rate me as a (husband, wife, partner, etc.) this past week?"

If it's not a ten ask, "What would I have to do different to get it up to a ten?"

If, however, you're not *both* committed to experiencing a successful, loving, and happy relationship, then you might want to do a "Ben Franklin close" on your current situation to see what percent of the time you are happy and what percent of the time you are unhappy and consider your options. You can't do it alone. It takes *both* of you committing 100 percent each to have a successful, happy, and mutually fulfilling relationship. Life is too long *not* to be happy.

WRIGHT

What can I do to help other people be happy?

HUMES

Be happy yourself. We teach by example, whether we want to or not. Be an example of happiness for others.

Have you ever met someone and became totally enthralled by him or her and you wanted to know what that person knew?

In 1986, a close friend and I visited a man in San Francisco, California. We ended up spending over six hours talking with him. I was fascinated by the way he communicated. I was curious about how he structured his thoughts in order to communicate so powerfully. I wanted to know what he knew about thinking and communicating. Near the end of our meeting I asked him a strange question, "What technology are you using to think?" He referred me to the classic general semantics book, *Science and Sanity,* by Alfred Korzybski, and NeuroLinguistic Programming (NLP) co-created by Richard Bandler and John Grinder. He gave me a list of books to read.

I was so blown away by NLP technology that I subsequently became a Certified NLP Practitioner in 1989. The reason I wanted to master NLP is because I saw it as the tool to help me master my mind and emotions so that I could be more consistently "on" as a professional drummer. I tell people that the difference between an amateur and a professional musician is that amateurs play great when they feel great; professionals play great no matter how they feel. NLP has helped me in many other areas in my life, especially in mastering my emotions.

So, I was greatly helped by a man because of his exceptional example of excellent communicating and thinking.

Everyone is an example. I've had many great and wonderful mentors, teachers, and gurus in my life. What I have discovered is that they are all fallible human beings. But that doesn't mean you should "throw out the baby with the bath water."

I think we were given a brain to use and to think for ourselves and not behave like "sheeple." Do your research and get information from as many different sources as possible, and then make up your own mind, rather than dogmatically, blindly following any one mentor, teacher, or guru.

Then, through *your* example, you will be successful at helping other people live a happy life.

WRIGHT

What got you involved in the business of happiness?

HUMES

In 1980 I heard my very first "success education" cassette tape. It was a program called "The Psychology of Winning," by Dr. Denis Waitley. I'm honored and humbled, by the way, to be in this book with Dr. Waitley now. That recording totally changed my life. I never knew that there was such a thing as a "psychology of winning." At the time I was a professional drummer and remember saying to myself, "I could see myself being a professional speaker when I'm around the age of fifty."

I prefer to have a vocation that I'm passionate about *and* that's fun. In 1999 the music business stopped being fun for me, so I decided to make a change. After a lot of soul-searching and career counseling, I decided to follow the vision I had years ago and become a professional speaker.

My personal purpose/mission statement is, "To inspire the best in myself and others to grow mentally, evolve in consciousness/awareness, and experience sustained eudemonic happiness." Since human beings ultimately want to be happy and avoid being unhappy, I thought, why not teach happiness?

After years of research, facilitating happiness workshops/meetups, constant refining, and modeling extremely happy people, I've developed and facilitate an intensive, interactive two-day program called *The Happiness Workshop* (www.TheHappinessWorkshop.com).

More businesses are finally beginning to understand the importance of having a happy workforce. Happier employees give better customer service, take fewer sick days, reduce health care expenses, stay at their jobs longer, and are more productive. I've adapted *The Happiness Workshop* for businesses with a program called *Happiness In The Workplace* (HappinessInTheWorkplace.com).

For the *nuptially challenged*, I facilitate a *Rebuilding Workshop*, which meets one night a week for ten weeks (www.HappinessAfterDivorce.org). Graduates of this educational workshop learn about the different phases people typically go through after the ending of a love relationship. They are more capable of building and creating lasting and healthy relationships in the future. It is designed to help participants turn his or her personal crisis into a creative transformational experience, which turns their stumbling blocks into rebuilding blocks—or *steppingstones*—for living a happy life.

DAVID HUMES, CHt. is a happiness coach and workshop facilitator. He is a professional member of the National Speakers Association (NSA), the past president of NSA Tennessee (NSAT), and was voted NSAT Chapter Member of the Year three times by his peers. He is a Certified Hypnotherapist, a Certified NLP Practitioner, an ordained minister, and an internationally certified second degree black belt in Wado-Ryu karate.

David has presented over eight hundred full day seminars to thousands of attendees in forty-eight states and throughout Canada for clients that include Verizon, DirecTV, Johns Hopkins University, ITT Technical Institute, and many others.

As a professional drummer, David had the privilege of performing with Timothy B. Schmit (Eagles), Lyle Workman (Sting), and Myron Dove (Santana) among others. He opened concerts for George Strait, Alan Jackson, Merle Haggard, Alabama, and many others.

DAVID HUMES, CHT
P.O. Box 450
Antioch, TN 37011
(615) 399-9164
info@TheHappinessWorkshop.com
www.TheHappinessWorkshop.com
Blog: www.Happy23-7.com

CHAPTER FIVE

Discover Your Inner Resource

AN INTERVIEW WITH.... DR. DEEPAK CHOPRA

DAVID WRIGHT (WRIGHT)

Today we are talking to Dr. Deepak Chopra, founder of the Chopra Center for Well Being in Carlsbad, California. More than a decade ago, Dr. Chopra became the foremost pioneer in integrated medicine. His insights have redefined our definition of health to embrace body, mind and spirit. His books, which include, *Quantum Healing, Perfect Health, Ageless Body Timeless Mind*, and *The Seven Spiritual Laws of Success,* have become international bestsellers and are established classics.

Dr. Chopra, welcome to *Stepping Stones to Success.*

DR. DEEPAK CHOPRA (CHOPRA)

Thank you. How are you?

WRIGHT

I am doing just fine. It's great weather here in Tennessee.

CHOPRA

Great.

WRIGHT

Dr. Chopra, you stated in your book, *Grow Younger, Live Longer: 10 Steps to Reverse Aging,* that it is possible to reset your biostats up to fifteen years younger than your chronological age. Is that really possible?

CHOPRA

Yes. There are several examples of this. The literature on aging really began to become interesting in the 1980s when people showed that it was possible to reverse the biological marks of aging. This included things like blood pressure, bone density, body temperature, regulation of the metabolic rate, and other things like cardiovascular conditioning, cholesterol levels, muscle mass and strength of muscles, and even things like hearing, vision, sex hormone levels, and immune function.

One of the things that came out of those studies was that psychological age had a great influence on biological age. So you have three kinds of aging: chronological age is when you were born, biological age is what your biomarker shows, and psychological age is what your biostat says.

WRIGHT

You call our prior conditioning a prison. What do you mean?

CHOPRA

We have certain expectations about the aging process. Women expect to become menopausal in their early forties. People think they should retire at the age of sixty-five and then go Florida and spend the rest of their life in so-called retirement. These expectations actually influence the very biology of aging. What we call normal aging is actually the hypnosis of our social conditioning. If you can bypass that social conditioning, then you're free to reset your own biological clock.

WRIGHT

Everyone told me that I was supposed to retire at sixty-five. I'm somewhat older than that and as a matter of fact, today is my birthday.

CHOPRA

Well happy birthday. You know, the fact is that you should be having fun all the time and always feel youthful. You should always feel that you are contributing to society. It's not the retirement, but it's the passion with which you're involved in the well being of your society, your community, or the world at large.

WRIGHT

Great things keep happening to me. I have two daughters; one was born when I was fifty. That has changed my life quite a bit. I feel a lot younger than I am.

CHOPRA

The more you associate with young people, the more you will respond to that biological expression.

WRIGHT

Dr. Chopra, you suggest viewing our bodies from the perspective of quantum physics. That seems somewhat technical. Will you tell us a little bit more about that?

CHOPRA

You see, on one level, your body is made up of flesh and bone. That's the material level but we know today that everything we consider matter is born of energy and information. By starting to think of our bodies as networks of energy information and even intelligence, we begin to shift our perspective. We don't think of our bodies so much as dense matter, but as vibrations of consciousness. Even though it sounds technical, everyone has had an experience with this so-called quantum body. After, for example, you do an intense workout, you feel a sense of energy in your body—a tingling sensation. You're actually experiencing what ancient wisdom traditions call the "vital force." The more you pay attention to this vital force inside your body, the more you will experience it as energy, information, and intelligence, and the more control you will have over its expressions.

WRIGHT

Does DNA have anything to do with that?

CHOPRA

DNA is the source of everything in our body. DNA is like the language that creates the molecules of our bodies. DNA is like a protein-making factory, but DNA doesn't give us the blueprint. When I build a house, I have to go to the factory to find the bricks, but having the bricks is not enough. I need to get an architect, who in his or her consciousness can create that blueprint. And that blueprint exists only in your spirit and consciousness—in your soul.

WRIGHT

I was interested in a statement from your book. You said that perceptions create reality. What perceptions must we change in order to reverse our biological image?

CHOPRA

You have to change three perceptions. First you have to get rid of the perceptions of aging itself. Most people believe that aging means disease and infirmities. You have to change that. You have to regard aging as an opportunity for personal growth and spiritual growth. You also have to regard it as an opportunity to express the wisdom of your experience and an opportunity to help others and lift them from ordinary and mundane experience to the kind of experiences you are capable of because you have much more experience than they do.

The second thing you have to change your perception of is your physical body. You have to start to experience it as information and energy—as a network of information and intelligence.

The third thing you have to change your perception on is the experience of dying. If you are the kind of person who is constantly running out of time, you will continue to run out of time. On the other hand, if you have a lot of time, and if you do everything with gusto and love and passion, then you will lose track of time. When you lose track of time, your body does not metabolize that experience.

WRIGHT

That is interesting. People who teach time management don't really teach the passion.

CHOPRA

No, no. Time management is such a restriction of time. Your biological clock starts to age much more rapidly. I think what you have to really do is live your life with passion so that time doesn't mean anything to you.

WRIGHT

That's a concept I've never heard.

CHOPRA

Well, there you are.

WRIGHT

You spend an entire chapter of your book on deep rest as an important part of the reversal of the aging process. What is "deep rest"?

CHOPRA

One of the most important mechanisms for renewal and survival is sleep. If you deprive an animal of sleep, then it ages very fast and dies prematurely. We live in a culture where most of our population has to resort to sleeping pills and tranquilizers in order to sleep. That doesn't bring natural rejuvenation and renewal. You know that you have had a good night's sleep when you wake up in the morning, feeling renewed, invigorated, and refreshed — like a baby does. So that's one kind of deep rest. That comes from deep sleep and from natural sleep. In the book I talk about how you go about making sure you get that.

The second deep rest comes from the experience of meditation, which is the ability to quiet your mind so you still your internal dialogue. When your internal dialogue is still, then you enter into a stage of deep rest. When your mind is agitated, your body is unable to rest.

WRIGHT

I have always heard of people who had bad eyesight and really didn't realize it until they went to the doctor and were fitted for lenses. I had that same experience some years ago. For several years I had not really enjoyed the deep sleep you're talking about. The doctor diagnosed me with sleep apnea. Now I sleep like a baby, and it makes a tremendous difference.

CHOPRA

Of course it does. You now have energy and the ability to concentrate and do things.

WRIGHT

Dr. Chopra, how much do eating habits have to do with aging? Can we change and reverse our biological age by what we eat?

CHOPRA

Yes, you can. One of the most important things to remember is that certain types of foods actually contain anti-aging compounds. There are many chemicals that are contained in certain foods that have an anti-aging effect. Most of these chemicals are derived from light. There's no way to bottle them—there are no pills you can take that will give you these chemicals. But they're contained in plants that are rich in color and derived from photosynthesis. Anything that is yellow, green, and red or has a lot of color, such as fruits and vegetables, contain a lot of these very powerful anti-aging chemicals.

In addition, you have to be careful not to put food in your body that is dead or has no life energy. So anything that comes in a can or has a label, qualifies for that. You have to expose your body to six tastes: sweet, sour, salt, bitter, pungent, and astringent because those are the codes of intelligence that allow us to access the deep intelligence of nature. Nature and what she gives to us in bounty is actually experienced through the sense of taste. In fact, the light chemicals—the anti-aging substances in food—create the six tastes.

WRIGHT

Some time ago, I was talking to one of the ladies in your office and she sent me an invitation to a symposium that you had in California. I was really interested. The title was *Exploring the Reality of Soul*.

CHOPRA

Well, I conducted the symposium, but we had some of the world's scientists, physicists, and biologists who were doing research in what is called, non-local intelligence—the intelligence of soul or spirit. You could say it is the intelligence that orchestrates the activity of the universe—God, for example. Science and spirituality are now meeting together because by understanding how nature works and how the laws of nature work, we're beginning to get a glimpse of a deeper intelligence that people in spiritual traditions call divine, or God. I think this is a wonderful time to explore spirituality through science.

WRIGHT

She also sent me biographical information of the seven scientists that were with you. I have never read a list of seven more noted people in their industry.

CHOPRA

They are. The director of the Max Planck Institute, in Berlin, Germany, where quantum physics was discovered was there. Dr. Grossam was a professor of physics at the University of Oregon, and he talked about the quantum creativity of death and the survival of conscious after death. It was an extraordinary group of people.

WRIGHT

Dr. Chopra, with our *Stepping Stones to Success* book we're trying to encourage people to be better, live better, and be more fulfilled by listening to the examples of our guest authors. Is there anything or anyone in your life who has made a difference for you and has helped you to become a better person?

CHOPRA

The most important person in my life was my father. Every day he asked himself, "What can I do in thought, word, and deed to nurture every relationship I encounter just for today?" That has lived with me for my entire life.

WRIGHT

What do you think makes up a great mentor? Are there characteristics mentors seem to have in common?

CHOPRA

I think the most important attribute of a great mentor is that he or she teaches by example and not necessarily through words.

WRIGHT

When you consider the choices you've made down through the years, has faith played an important role?

CHOPRA

I think more than faith, curiosity, wonder, a sense of reference, and humility has. Now, if you want to call that faith, then, yes it has.

WRIGHT

In a divine being?

CHOPRA

In a greater intelligence—intelligence that is supreme, infinite, unbounded, and too mysterious for the finite mind to comprehend.

WRIGHT

If you could have a platform and tell our audience something you feel would help them and encourage them, what would you say?

CHOPRA

I would say that there are many techniques that come to us from ancient wisdom and tradition that allow us to tap into our inner resources and allow us to become beings who have intuition, creativity, vision, and a connection to that which is sacred. Finding that within ourselves, we have the means to enhance our well-being. Whether it's physical, emotional, or environmental, we have the means to resolve conflicts and get rid of war. We have the means to be really healthy. We have the means for being economically uplifted. That knowledge is the most important knowledge that exists.

WRIGHT

I have seen you on several primetime television shows down through the years where you have had the time to explain your theories and beliefs. How does someone like me experience this? Do we get it out of books?

CHOPRA

Books are tools that offer you a road map. Sit down every day, close your eyes, put your attention in your heart, and ask yourself two questions: who am I and what do I want? Then maintain a short period of stillness in body and mind as in prayer or meditation, and the door will open.

WRIGHT

So, you think that the intelligence comes from within. Do all of us have that capacity?

CHOPRA

Every child born has that capacity.

WRIGHT

That's fascinating. So, it doesn't take trickery or anything like that?

CHOPRA

No, it says in the Bible in the book of Psalms, *"Be still and know that I am God" – Psalm 46:10.*

WRIGHT

That's great advice.

I really do appreciate your being with us today. You are fascinating. I wish I could talk with you for the rest of the afternoon. I'm certain I am one of millions who would like to do that!

CHOPRA

Thank you, sir. It was a pleasure to talk with you!

WRIGHT

Today we have been talking with Dr. Deepak Chopra, founder of The Chopra Center. He has become the foremost pioneer in integrated medicine. We have found today that he really knows what he's talking about. After reading his book, *Grow Younger, Live Longer: 10 Steps to Reverse Aging,* I can tell you that I highly recommend it. I certainly hope you'll go out to your favorite book store and buy a copy.

Dr. Chopra, thank you so much for being with us today on *Stepping Stones to Success.*

CHOPRA

Thank you for having me, David.

Deepak Chopra has written more than fifty books, which have been translated into many languages. He is also featured on many audio and videotape series, including five critically acclaimed programs on public television. He has also written novels and edited collections of spiritual poetry from India and Persia. In 1999, *Time* magazine selected Dr. Chopra as one of the Top 100 Icons and Heroes of the Century, describing him and "the poet-prophet of alternative medicine."

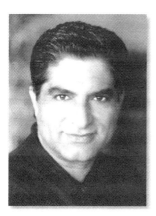

DR. DEEPAK CHOPRA
The Chopra Center
2013 Costa del Mar Rd.
Carlsbad, CA 92009
info@chopra.com
www.chopra.com

CHAPTER SIX

Networking to Enhance Your Life's Purpose

AN INTERVIEW WITH.... PAT CHILDERS

DAVID WRIGHT (WRIGHT)

Today we're talking with Pat Childers. Pat is a successful life coach who has been working with all types of individuals and groups her entire life with the sole purpose of raising the energy of consciousness so everyone has the opportunity to be successful. Her goal in life is to assist each person she works with to achieve whatever it is they truly want. She is President and Founder of the Empowerment Network and has worked with executives in her local area as well as traveling all over the country assisting with many events utilizing her networking skills.

Pat Childers, welcome to *Stepping Stones to Success*.

PAT CHILDERS (CHILDERS)

Thank you very much, David.

WRIGHT

So where can people network for success?

CHILDERS

The way I see it, anywhere and everywhere. From standing in line at the grocery store to huge business conventions, life allows each individual the opportunity to network with "all connections."

WRIGHT

So how should people be prepared to network?

CHILDERS

By knowing exactly what they really want and need, and being ready to assist others in their desires as well.

WRIGHT

I remember telling a speaker one time, if he went into Kroger today, and walked up and down every aisle, how many people will stop you and ask you a question? The answer was "None." I said, "Well, what about if you stand in line with a ball cap on that says, 'I am a public speaker;' how many people are going to ask you then? He said, "I think a few might."

CHILDERS

Well, I have the experience, whether I have the hat on or not. People ask me *lots* of questions, wherever I am.

WRIGHT

So what type of interaction feels most comfortable while networking?

CHILDERS

Connecting with "attention" for one thing, and being organized by knowing what you really want and need, so you're open to the positive results you will get in return with each encounter.

WRIGHT

So what value or service can be shared while you're networking?

CHILDERS

The way I look at it is staying true to who each individual is by contributing to his or her highest knowledge, while enhancing his or her assets and content material by creating and living the dream. The person who is talking to each "one" needs to be aware that everybody can help. Each person has individual strengths for connecting for a higher purpose in all matters

WRIGHT

So, in your opinion, what is the best way to present oneself while networking?

CHILDERS

It's not who you know, but who knows you. The first thing you need to do is make a good impression and a lasting impression on people. It's important to be true to yourself when you do that. When you make a favorable impression, you have good results in return and you can communicate with confidence at all times.

WRIGHT

So, after making a fabulous connection with someone, then what?

CHILDERS

Then it's a good idea to do follow-up. You can call people if you've gotten their numbers, you can e-mail them, or send them thank-you cards if they've given you a good contact, and then you can even get together for a dinner later, just because it was fun and you enjoy them.

WRIGHT

So where am I taking my networking results in the future?

CHILDERS

Well, I've made fabulous connections with authors, business owners, and coaches across the country. That's what my objective is—to go back out there and speak, so the people will understand what would be the most prosperous, most helpful, and would make them the happiest.

WRIGHT

Consider that I'm a reader of this book, *Stepping Stones to Success*, and people have been talking to me about networking. I've known what it is on the fringe, but how do I start? Do you have any tips on the kinds of things I can do or learn that would help me develop the attitude of a great networker?

CHILDERS

It's good to have your thoughts organized on what it is you really need. You can pay attention to how the people are responding to you, and you'll know how far to go with that. It's always good to have an agenda ready, but not to be obvious about it. Your agenda is inside you, so you are making good contacts for what you can help them with and how they can help you.

WRIGHT

You're saying my contacts will help me and I can help them. Networking is a reciprocal agreement. How does that work?

CHILDERS

For instance, you can go to different places that you know you have a connection, like certain organizations and meetings, conventions, class reunions, etc. and you never know for sure who you're going to see again. You can also set up Web sites on the Internet and say, "I'm looking for whatever you need." You will have people call back or send something back to you. Volunteer work is a wonderful opportunity to connect. Continuing education classes give you the chance to enhance your knowledge to assist with what you really want to do and you can make connections there too.

WRIGHT

I remember someone years ago saying to me, "If my wife would pay more attention to me I would take her flowers," I told him, "You know, you might want to try taking the flowers first." So is that the way networking works? Do you try to help other people to get them to help you?

CHILDERS

It's a really good way to be. It's not that you're out there manipulating or being selfish by saying, "Oh, I'm going to do this, so they will do that for me." It's that you really want to. You get yourself in the frame of mind that says, "Hey, I know that person is interested in this, I'll take him [or her] that." Then the person will see, and can connect with what it was you connected with for the person.

WRIGHT

In your experience has networking been ongoing? If someone helps you or refers someone to your services or helps you sell one of your products, is the probability higher that the person will do it again?

CHILDERS

Yes, especially if you have a good relationship with the person and he or she understands that you're being honest and sincere in what your objectives are.

People get excited about it too, and they think of another person, "Oh, that will help this one, and that will help this one. Oh, this company could really use that product." So they get excited too, and then you can do the same for them.

WRIGHT

So, what is the message I want people to hear so they can learn from my success?

CHILDERS

My personal message to everyone is, "It's never too late to live your dream, your passion and your joy." Some people think, "Oh I'm sixty, seventy, or eighty years old, I can't do anything anymore, I'm just this and that." Some people think, "Oh, I'm not prepared; I don't understand." But you can always search and find your dream and live it!

WRIGHT

So, how can we all help each other succeed?

CHILDERS

By being open to recognizing what assets you have that could help the other person, and then recognize what the other person has that can help you. It's very much an "open heart institution." Live the life by being that way.

WRIGHT

You've mentioned being honest and sincere earlier in this conversation—that must really be important.

CHILDERS

It is, because you don't want to be known as someone who is just working somebody for the heck of it or for your own gain. You want to be really sincere. You'll then be well-known and admired. People will come to you and say, "Hey, I've got an idea—" Who knows what kind of wonderful new relationship you can have or new business you can develop?

WRIGHT

So, if I join a Rotary Club or an Optimist Club, or a Civitan Club, would the people I meet there merely be in my network? What other reason would I have to join a club like these?

CHILDERS

You should look at what the club you want to join does and what it stands for. Ask yourself, "Hmm, will that benefit me in moving forward with what it is that I really need to do in the world?" Sometimes you want to go to those events just because it's fun to be with people. You never know who might join the same day you do, and there it is—there is your connection.

WRIGHT

It sounds to me as though I can make lasting friendships from people in a network.

CHILDERS

Yes, you really can!

WRIGHT

So, you're not talking strictly about business are you?

CHILDERS

Well, you know what, "It's nice to know that you can have new business contacts that are, and/or could become your friends."

WRIGHT

So, what does your network equal?

CHILDERS

Your network equals your net worth. And by letting others into your life and leading the way, you are loving people and hearing their stories. You're there for them while you still continue your dream, and stay true to yourself, thereby everyone wins by accomplishing their goals to success.

WRIGHT

Do you personally set networking goals? Is it a way of life for you and do you track them?

CHILDERS

Actually, David, you did tap into something for me. I have always done this. It has been my whole life, even when I was in grade school. People would come up to me, and I would network for them, and I would say, "Oh, this one is doing the game over there," and "Oh, I can tell you about that—" I've always helped people—it's something that I've always done and it's who I am."

WRIGHT

So, this is life for you—you don't have to track it.

CHILDERS

No, but if you have a particular project you're really working on, it's good to write it down, and ask, "Okay, what is my goal right now? Where am I going, and what's my objective?" So those are good things to do as well.

WRIGHT

What if some of our readers are shy and reticent—what if they haven't had the kind of experiences you have had, but they do believe in networking and want to do it—what do they do?

CHILDERS

Everyone has strengths. What people need to do for themselves is look inside, and ask, "What are my true strengths that I can help someone else with?" Then, as they show those, they will make contacts recognizing who they really are instead of just hiding behind their shyness.

WRIGHT

When someone in your network does something that is good for you—gives you a client or a referral—how important is it to give him or her feedback? Is that part of the system?

CHILDERS

I believe it's part of the system, and it is also sharing. People can benefit from feedback and they'll know, "Oh my gosh, I really helped." They can see what idea comes from what they suggested. It's not even a bad idea—if you feel like it from your heart—to give them something, just because. It doesn't have to be a contact, it can be some gift, like flowers, a book, or whatever. It doesn't have to be huge, just nice.

WRIGHT

So what's up next for Pat Childers? What's coming up for you? Do you have any plans to do anything new in your coaching business? How is that going?

CHILDERS

Actually I do. I have a book inside me that is ready to be written as the dissertation for my doctorate. Then I'm going to connect with a lot of the students, because the name of my book is *The Indigo Grandmother: Communication Among the Generations.* Since I was a teacher in the past, I want to go back out and connect with a lot of the college kids who are sitting on the fence right now, and do some talks and make some connections with them as well, so that they'll be ready to go out and live their own life.

WRIGHT

I read in your biography that you work with all types of individuals and groups and have for a long time with the sole purpose of raising the "energy of consciousness." What is that?

CHILDERS

What that means is people are really good—it's just that sometimes they've had lots of consequences and lots of stop signs and other problems that have put them in a different place, and they haven't been living their full self. Living a life to their fullest potential will connect them to more people in a positive way. When that happens, we can all have a better world. That's what I mean!

I'm excited and looking forward to connecting with any and all groups, to enhance the connection, and to raise the consciousness of the world.

WRIGHT

Do you really believe that everyone has the opportunity to be successful?

CHILDERS

Yes, I do. I believe that everybody has different goals and different plans. Someone could be a successful stock boy at the store, but if that makes him happy, well then, he's doing what he's here to do. You could be a successful librarian at the school, or you could be anything. If what you're doing makes you happy, and if it is what you really want, then you're living your life purpose.

WRIGHT

Interesting. As a matter of fact, all of these answers have been interesting. I really appreciate all this time you've spent with me to answer these questions.

CHILDERS

I appreciate talking with you.

WRIGHT

I've learned a lot and I think our readers will too.

CHILDERS

I've enjoyed speaking with you. Thank you very much for the opportunity to share.

WRIGHT

Today we've been talking with Pat Childers who is a successful life coach and President and Founder of the Empowerment Network. Her goal in life is to assist each person she works with to achieve whatever it is he or she truly wants. I think I might call her and see if she can help me. That sounds like a good goal.

Pat, thank you so much for being with us today for this interview for *Stepping Stones to Success.*

CHILDERS

Thank you very much David. I'm very excited to have had our conversation.

PAT CHILDERS is a doctoral candidate whose dissertation is her book, *The Indigo Grandmother: Communication Among the Generations.* She holds Bachelor's and Master's degrees in education, and also has her certification to teach gifted and talented students. She has taught in junior high, high school, and college.

Pat enjoys sharing information through the written word, and has contributed to two other anthologies, *Conscious Entrepreneurs: A Radical New Approach to Purpose, Passion, and Profit,* and *The Indigo Children: Ten Years Later,* as well as newspaper and magazine articles. She also enjoys sharing information on TV, radio, live lectures, and individual sessions.

She lives a full life as a minister, teacher, healer, lecturer, mom, grandma, life coach, promoter, networker, and event coordinator. She is looking forward to continuing reaching many people by connecting to a variety of venues when speaking at seminars and conferences across the country.

PAT CHILDERS

1022 Roanoke Lane
Marshfield, MO 65706
417-859-4963
patchilders1111@yahoo.com
www.patchilders.com

CHAPTER SEVEN

Create Your Perfect Life

DAVID WRIGHT (WRIGHT)

Today we're talking with Katana Abbott. Katana is founder and vision coach of MidlifeMillionaires.com and upcoming author of *Secrets from a Midlife Millionaire.* She retired in the top one percent of money managers nationwide following twenty years as a senior financial advisor for Ameriprise Financial. Today, she is following her passion by helping others reach their midlife millionaire goals. She provides wealth-building know-how that will allow them to achieve financial independence and live the life of their dreams. A Certified Financial Planner and Certified Senior Advisor, Katana also is the founder of SmartWomensCoaching.com, SmartWomensCafe.com, and the nonprofit, Smart Women's Empowerment Program.

Katana, welcome to *Stepping Stones to Success.*

Why did you create MidifeMillionaires.com?

KATANA ABBOTT (ABBOTT)

For twenty years, I helped men and women navigate their way to financial independence and wealth. But while I was focusing on the nuts and bolts of financial planning, I discovered that so many people—even those who achieve financial security—are not living the life of their dreams. They are not following their true passions.

Creating wealth and an ongoing source of income can create that freedom to pursue your real passions—whether it's to start your own business, live and play on an exotic island, write a book, join the Peace Corps, or change the world in other ways.

My passion was not just to become wealthy. I did that. My passion was to help others follow their passion. With MidlifeMillionaires.com, I can focus on both the financial and lifestyle goals of my clients and readers. I was able to gather a formidable array of experts, too, with my fellow coaches and contributing experts who can address so many facets of what makes up that word "Success."

Success is never just about the money—it's about achieving that feeling of joy, abundance, and fulfillment. MidlifeMillionaires.com was my Eureka. It is my passion—my inspiration. Now I am able to help others follow their steppingstones to success.

WRIGHT

You also are the founder, principal, and vision coach of SmartWomensCoaching.com. Why did you decide to create this special focus on women?

ABBOTT

I've always wanted to create a special program for women, who often face so many layers of challenges such as caretakers on top of their careers, for example. As a woman who overcame so many obstacles that women face—poverty, abuse, and glass ceilings. I know how to incorporate all those roles and challenges in helping women build wealth and achieve their dreams. I did it for twenty years with Ameriprise Financial, but in that role I only addressed the financial aspects of their lives.

With Smart Women's Coaching, I can address both the financial and lifestyle needs of women. I also can reach out to more women through the worldwide reach of the Internet.

It's a holistic approach on how to master business, life, and relationships, with special appeal to women of any age. The success of Smart Women's Coaching led me to recently create a worldwide network for professional women and entrepreneurs called Smart Women's Café. SmartWomensCafe.com provides twenty-four-hour access to smart advice, information, and learning opportunities in a very informal setting.

Of course, men are invited. This is an inclusive outreach that includes male and female experts offering their unique expertise in this one-stop-shopping venue for education, motivation, inspiration, and networking.

WRIGHT

Since you already have helped so many men and women over more than two decades, is there any common denominator when it comes to what holds people back and what propels them forward to success?

ABBOTT

I have a trademarked way I guide men and women from all walks of life. I call it "starting from smart" or "starting from scratch." The first group has accumulated wealth, but they are not pursuing a life with purpose. My goal with these individuals is to channel their finances and continue wealth-building opportunities which will free up their time and mindset to pursue their true passions in life while accumulating income. They're starting from smart, but not from their heart.

Of course, the majority of people are in the second group, and starting from scratch. They have not taken the smart financial steps to building wealth. Or the current economy has pushed them off the success track. They have been laid off, the cost of living is rising, or they have lost their retirement savings due to the recent crashes on Wall Street. My goal with these individuals is to help them build their confidence about their current situation, to take stock of where they are and get very clear about their goals, values and strengths. Going through this process with a mentor, coach or financial advisor can be all someone needs to get back on track to financial and life success.

What I find many people have in common is fear of stepping outside their comfort zone. I know, because I've had to jump that hurdle, too. I have lived a life that took me from "adversity to abundance." I was poor—too poor to continue my college studies—and I was living with an abusive husband. I left him and worked my way up to join the top echelons of successful financial planners. But the fear that came from having lived with nothing and survived so much pain made me afraid to take that next step in my career.

It's funny what happened next to me. Here I was, at the top of my game. My business was running virtually without me and I knew it was time to move on. I was in a situation where I had all these creative ideas and because of my relationship with my Ameriprise franchise agreement and the added regulations of the SEC, I was unable to pursue most of my creative endeavors in my current role as financial advisor. I was forced to make a decision: Would I maintain my current financial security and just snuff out my dreams? It was at that moment when I had to overcome that fear to be able to reach my success as a midlife millionaire, and then start over again to build my new business and my new network pursuing my real passion.

You just have to ask yourself what you really want. Is what you want worth overcoming your fear? Even if you take tiny steps at first, you must take that first step and walk through that door, because when you do, that's where you will find your power.

Here is an exercise that I find really helpful. Envision your perfect life three years from now: What would you be doing? Where would you be living and with whom? Then journal about this and begin to write out what would have to happen over the next three years to make that a reality.

This is the simple process I use to help individuals become very clear about where they want to go so that they can begin to create their written goals. These are the steppingstones that will lead to your success. They are laid out in a direct line to your goal. Recognize your fear, acknowledge your fear, and create a plan that gives you the confidence and inspiration to take one step, and then another, and then another.

WRIGHT

Why are traditional retirement plans no longer an option for so many people? Why do they need to create new steppingstones to success, even at midlife, a time when past generations were winding down their careers?

ABBOTT

Retirement is no longer an option for many people at midlife, whether for financial reasons or because they don't want to wind down. Many people at this age are thinking, "What can I do right now to start over and pursue my real passions and talents? How can I make that possible?"

A June 2008 *Associated Press* survey reports that 66 percent of Baby Boomers expect to continue working after "retiring." According to a 2008 survey by NAVA, the Association for Insured Retirement Solutions, only 21 percent of Baby Boomers believe they have done an excellent job saving for retirement.

Even those Boomers with adequate savings will, in coming years, have more reason to revisit their financial strategies. For example, a three-university study in 2008 for the American Association of Retired Persons (AARP) found that the rate of bankruptcy filings by Americans ages sixty-five and older doubled between 1991 and 2007.

Unplanned medical costs were responsible for the majority of these bankruptcy filings. This and lower home values are erasing the advantages of the generation that came before the Boomers. That generation enjoyed stronger home equity, greater savings, and a stronger financial cushion of traditional pensions.

Traditional pensions have since diminished as a source of retirement income for Boomers, and even more so for post-Baby Boom generations. Most companies no longer offer traditional pensions, and fewer are offering attractive 401(k) programs either.

According to the Employment Benefit Research Institute, more than one in three workers ages thirty-five to forty-four aren't setting aside money for retirement. Among those ages twenty-five to thirty-four, 45 percent are not saving.

The Center for Retirement Research at Boston College has calculated that nearly half (48 percent) of the forty-nine million members of Generation X are at a high risk of being unable to maintain their standard of living upon retirement.

Lifestyle needs also have changed. For example, of the forty-five million Baby Boomer women at a midlife crossroads, many are struggling with working full-time, raising a family, caring for elderly parents, hampered by divorce or widowhood, or struggling to face a future with no real financial safety net.

Yet, there is a powerful shift at play as some women transition from their childbearing years and emerge into a time of renewed creativity and freedom.

At the same time, studies show that some men expect to downshift their energies as they reach retirement.

The goal is to be flexible in finding your steppingstones for success. Know that there will be economic ups and downs, just as there will be ups and downs in your personal life. A smart plan will allow for contingencies and build a wealth platform that will provide its own cushion to those ups and downs. The goal, again, is to make your steppingstones in a straight line toward your goal. If you stray from those steppingstones, just get back on the path.

WRIGHT

What do you suggest individuals do to supplement their retirement plans, given what's been happing in the economy these last several years?

ABBOTT

I used to say retirement was a three-legged stool made up of pension, social security, and personal savings. Now I think we need to add another leg to the stool—inspirational, lifelong work to create an ongoing stream of income. I help my clients learn how to create passive income that will continue to accrue throughout their lives, even when they might be unable or unwilling to work anymore.

When you think about personal savings, it can be in the form of CDs and brokerage accounts. However, most retirement savings will be in the form of deferred compensation plans, and the most popular are in the form of an IRA (Individual Retirement Account) or a 401(k).

The secret to building this type of retirement plan is starting early to take advantage of the "time-value" of money. For example, to save $1 million by age sixty-five (assuming a very generous 10 percent annual rate of return), take a look at the different amounts an individual would need to save, depending on how late he or she began to save:

Age	Daily Savings	Yearly Savings
20	$4.00	$1,460
30	$11.11	$4,015
40	$30.00	$10,950
50	$95.00	$34,675

As you can see, starting early is the key here, so encourage your children to start saving for retirement as soon as they reach adulthood. But what does this mean for people who are now forty or fifty and do not have a pension, a large 401(k), or IRA plan? How will they ever retire to follow their passion? Where will this income come from? What will happen if they become ill or disabled?

Even if you had $1 million invested in an IRA or 401(k) plan, how much do you think you would be able to pull out of it over thirty years without running out of money—5 percent, 7 percent, 10 percent? Based on conservative financial planning assumptions, you would only want to take out 4 percent per year based on a balanced portfolio of stocks and bonds and, considering market volatility, adjusting for taxes and inflation. Do you have any idea how much this would mean in the way of weekly income? You could expect around $770 per week before taxes.

Now let's consider that you are somewhere between forty and fifty right now, and you are not even close to reaching your goal of $1 million in your retirement portfolio by age sixty-five. Which of these options might be a more realistic way to generate $770 per week for thirty years: saving $10,000 to $35,000 per year in a pre-tax retirement portfolio, or starting a business based on your unique skills, talents, hobbies, and passions? Also ask yourself what would bring you more fulfillment, enjoyment, and potential for even more income? I believe starting a business makes the most sense.

WRIGHT

You also have a time management system that you have been using for years that is part of your steppingstones to success. How does your time management system work?

ABBOTT

Part of creating a millionaire lifestyle is managing your life and your daily calendar so that you can be effective, stay inspired, and can create an ongoing, lifetime passive income. It all starts with creating your Perfect Life Calendar. This is a critical step, since your calendar will provide you a system to manage your time, focus, and energies. Without this structure, you may find yourself overwhelmed and disorganized—a sure path to failure.

My signature Perfect Life Calendar incorporates three categories of days: Power Days, Prep Days, and Perfect Days. The goal is this:

- Increase your productivity and earning potential on your Power Days.
- Improve your level of energy, focus, and clarity by cleaning up messes and getting very organized on your Prep Days.
- Make more time for yourself, your friends, and your family by scheduling and enjoying wonderful Perfect Days!

Now you have the basis for this time system. I begin by planning my Perfect Days first. I plan my vacations and personal time for my family, friends, and myself in advance so that I can stay rejuvenated. You never want to wait until you crash and burn or get sick to make time for yourself.

Next, I plan all the Prep Days that I will need to clean up messes, get organized, create systems, delegate, and outsource. You will have more of these when you start out, and less as your systems develop and you begin to outsource or delegate to others. Stephen Covey calls this "Quadrant 2 Activities."

The last days I plan are my Power Days. These are my Money Days—the days that I am focused on my unique abilities, talents, and passions. I will focus my entire day on things that I love doing, the things that I am great at, and that make me the most money.

What is remarkable is that when I follow this model, I end up with a very concrete number of Power Days. In fact, an interesting exercise I recommend is to count up all your Power Days for the year and divide that into the amount of money you plan to earn that year. This will give the dollar amount you are worth or should be earning each day or even each hour.

Your goal is to consistently follow your Perfect Week Calendar. Notify your staff, family, and friends so that you can work this schedule. You will be amazed how much more inspired and effective your life will become.

One other great benefit is that I gradually moved from fewer Power and Prep Days to more Perfect Days, with my Perfect Days often lasting weeks at a time. I can make a difference and empower other people, and still have as much time as I want to enjoy my personal life. I love my Perfect Life Calendar!

To reach that level of financial independence, I often advise clients to integrate passive income streams that will either become your life's passion or a become a way to create multiple income streams that will allow you to follow your true passion while building wealth. It's all about financial independence.

WRIGHT

What are some passive income streams that people can use as steppingstones to their success?

ABBOTT

One example would be a franchise. When I started my financial planning practice, I had purchased a franchise business. The company charged me an up-front "licensing fee," a monthly fee, and a percentage of my revenue. In return, I received access to American Express systems, processes, forms, accounting services, and reports, as well as the back room support of 5,000 office support employees, compliance attorneys, managers, and other resources. I had purchased a turnkey model plus the branding power that came with the name American Express.

When I decided to start Smart Women's Coaching after retiring at forty-eight, I had to start from the ground up. My new business embraces many different forms of passive income:

- Membership fees
- Licensing of products
- Affiliate fees for selling other products or referrals
- Coaching and consulting income
- Tuition for events, workshops, and tele-classes

- Speaking fees
- Product sales

As you can see, these are just several of the different types of income streams that can produce wealth for you by starting a franchise or starting your own business—if you do your homework. These are passive income generators that can become full-time, as my businesses did for me. However, with my new midlife millionaire lifestyle, my start-up business continues to produce income for me without my having to dedicate so many hours or days to it.

Most businesses fail because of a lack of homework, so I cannot emphasize enough that you do your homework and create a practical, smart plan. You will need to work with a team of advisors to do this correctly. Your team may consist of a financial advisor, attorney, CPA, business coach, bookkeeper, and administrative assistant.

Take a hard, honest look at where you stand right now financially. Then go to the expertise you can find through Web sites such as MidlifeMillionaires.com and SmartWomensCafe.com. The real power of the Internet is that there is such a wealth of expertise and experience represented by the people who make up the best Web-based networks. Plus, you can tap this expertise at any time and from any location.

At SmartWomensCafe.com, we created a community of experts who could provide the advice, services, and products demanded by our clients. We are leveraging our time and energy by offering group programs and membership programs, and from being paid for co-promoting and creating joint ventures. We are also leveraging technology by using the Internet and virtual assistants. The community we have created actually teaches you how to duplicate this process for yourself.

WRIGHT

What about the multi-level marketing (MLM) option for building wealth and continuing income streams? Can multi-level marketing become a steppingstone to success?

ABBOTT

Multi-level marketing is a passive income option also known as network marketing. There are all kinds of businesses that use this model to distribute their products. Here are just a few examples: Send Out Cards (a greeting card service), Two Sister Gourmet (food products), Arbonne (skin care products), Quick Star (Amway and online shopping mall), and YTB Travel (an on-line travel service)

I have had very positive experiences with MLM, but it is not for everyone. The biggest mistake is signing up for this type of business and then thinking you can do it your own way. The most important thing people can do with an MLM business is to work with their "up-line" — the person who brought them into the business — and follow all the proven strategies and systems that are already in place. You will fail if you try to do it your own way.

In June 2005, I became an Arbonne consultant while recovering from knee surgery. I paid $35, purchased some skin care products, printed up business cards, attended some meetings, and built a referral or "network marketing" business. I was paid a percentage of all the products I purchased (at a 35 percent discount) for my family and me. I also received a percentage of the sales of all the products purchased by anyone I referred to Arbonne. Better yet, I received a percentage of the price of all the products purchased by those additional people I had steered toward the product. This is why it is called multi-level marketing.

Many companies are using this model because it involves fewer start-up costs and it's very effective. Instead of paying millions of dollars in advertising, such companies rely on word-of-mouth advertising. Think about it: If you like a product, what do you do? You tell your friends. This is all you are doing in this type of business, except that the company you recommend then pays you a referral fee or commission.

These commissions can add up, too. Each month I was an Arbonne consultant, my paycheck doubled. I received a check for $4,500 in my sixth month. My sponsor, a regional vice president of the company, was receiving $10,000 a month, but she worked the business full-time.

Instead of pursuing a full-time career with Arbonne, I decided to focus on my start-up, Smart Women's Coaching. To this day, however, I continue to order my $100 worth of products every month (and only pay $65). I am still being paid for all those in my "down-line," the MLM term for those I signed up for the business. I regularly receive a check for $100 to $200, even though I have not been active for more than two years.

Unlike franchises and start-ups, MLM can prove a less expensive way to build passive income and can be started on a part-time basis. I call it having a Plan B. Even if an MLM business is not your ultimate passion, it can be a smart way to create passive income to achieve the financial independence to pursue your dream or a security blanket in case you lose your job. I earned more than $20,000 from Arbonne in 2007, even though I was not active in the business. I was able to use that income to fund my start-up business, Smart Women's Coaching!

The key to starting a network marketing or MLM business is finding one you are passionate about and then working very closely with the company you choose to implement the marketing and sales strategies that are already successful. Do your homework. Make a list on which the negatives match the positives to give you the smartest insights into whether multi-level marketing is a path you want to pursue on the way to your destination.

WRIGHT

Are there other options to help integrate wealth-building strategies into financial steppingstones to success?

ABBOTT

Many people have become successful as consultants and coaches. They have acquired expertise and translated that expertise into consulting services, books, coaching, and other opportunities.

There are drawbacks, of course. You could end up trading "dollars for hours." In other words, when you don't work, you don't get paid. Do you have enough financial resources or other streams of income to support you during those times you are not being paid?

As a consultant, *you* are the business. If you don't have a transition plan in place, you may not be able to sell your business or delegate its operations to others. Without multiple streams of income, you can generate by offering live classes, tele-classes, or products you create that "sell while you sleep," you are back to the "dollars for hours" trap.

However, coaching or consulting can prove a great part-time generator of passive income. Do your homework, and don't skip the math. What are others in your region charging for their services? Who would be your likely customers? These are the kinds of questions answered in a solid business plan. Before you take the plunge, create a business plan and consider hiring a business coach or working with a team of experts. It will be worth the investment.

WRIGHT

What about real estate, stocks, and bonds?

ABBOTT

Even in a depressed real estate sector and uneven stock market, there always are opportunities to create passive wealth that can become your steppingstones to success.

Real Estate can become passive income by renting homes or condominiums you own to regularly amass income from monthly rental payments. At a time of record foreclosures, many investors are buying homes individually as either second homes or as passive income generators. Simply put, they are becoming landlords. Many hire management companies to take care of the traditional landlord responsibilities, making their investments truly passive.

Another source of passive income is what's called "portfolio income." This is the interest and dividends derived from stocks, bonds, mutual funds, and other paper assets. Instead of planning on savings as the main source of passive income for retirement, consider it as a back-up to passive income businesses that grow wealth while you pursue your passion.

In any event, hire an outside expert to consult about passive income investments in real estate or paper assets. The risks to over-relying on real estate, stocks, and bonds became readily apparent on the front pages of every major newspaper in recent years in reports on tumbling real estate markets and the volatile stock market.

First, be cautious. Second, consult a professional. Third, do your homework.

WRIGHT

What about the time factor? How do people find the time to get to their destination?

ABBOTT

You have to make your destination—your true success—a priority. Yes, there are ways to increase your income, but is that what you really want? If so, be very clear about that with yourself. Do you want to use wealth-building opportunities to create your perfect life—a life of leisure, adventure, starting a business or changing the world? Be very clear with yourself that building wealth is one of many means to reach your "end" goal, based on how *you* define your success.

Once you are honest with yourself and confident in your choice of a destination in life, it becomes easier to create that time to achieve your goals. Look at how you spend every hour of your day and circle those hours that take you closer to your goal. Find a way to minimize or erase time spent on activities that don't move you closer to your goal. Keep that perfect life plan in front of you as your stepping-stone to success.

Cut out pictures and paste them on a Success Board to illustrate your perfect life. Write down your goals and affirmations on a piece of paper, and keep that piece of paper with you. Even leading personal development experts like Brian Tracy do these types of exercises. Brian re-writes his top ten goals every day. Writing and re-writing your goals help you focus on what you want, instead of what you don't want. Remember, we get what we focus on. You can be your own inspiration, and stay motivated, to avoid wasting time.

WRIGHT

What is your definition of your own success?

ABBOTT

I overcame many obstacles on my way to becoming a midlife millionaire and realizing my true passion in life. Those obstacles held me back with fear at first, and then made me stronger as I overcame each one.

I have a truly abundant life because I was able to incorporate my expertise at building wealth and financial security for others into building my own wealth, and then charting a new course that is even more rewarding. I am helping people achieve not just financial security and independence, but also to achieve their real dreams.

You really can leverage your time and energies to achieve fulfillment and happiness. I am grateful for so much, especially being able to play a role in helping others achieve their own vision of success. I now live a life with purpose. I now live My Perfect Life, one with purpose, passion and prosperity!

KATANA ABBOTT is founder and vision coach of MidlifeMillionaires.com and upcoming author of *Midlife Millionaire: Create Your Millionaire Lifestyle While Following Your Passion.* After retiring in the top one percent of money managers nationwide, following twenty years as a senior financial advisor for Ameriprise Financial, Abbott is following her passion. Abbott now helps others reach their midlife millionaire goals with wealth-building know-how that will allow them to achieve financial independence and live the life of their dreams. Abbott is a Certified Financial Planner and founder of SmartWomensCoaching.com, SmartWomensCafe.com, and the nonprofit Smart Women's Empowerment Program.

KATANA ABBOTT, CFP, CSA

Speaker, Author and Founder
3050 Union Lake Road, Suite 8F
Commerce, MI 48382
(248) 366-0137
Katana@MidlifeMillionaires.com
www.MidlifeMillionaires.com
www.SmartWomensCoaching.com
www.SmartWomensCafe.com

CHAPTER EIGHT

Leading by Giving

DAVID WRIGHT (WRIGHT)

Today we're talking with Mary Donohue, EdD. She an author, journalist and founder of the National Mentoring Program. Mary has worked in New York, San Francisco, and Toronto. She boasts a history of public relations, event planning, operations, and management as shown by rapid sales growth and advancement with such companies as MolsonCoors Canada (Molson), Red Bull, Honda, and Nike. Dr. Mary has a unique ability to create a sense of excitement and fun about her initiatives, motivating her clients and their customers to get fully engaged. She was described at a recent press conference by Paul Godfrey, former president of the Toronto Blue Jays Baseball Club, as a fireball and has been described by others as an idea tornado.

While learning about great leaders and ethics, Mary met and was moved to innovation by Paul Newman. Subsequently she completed her internship for her doctorate with Paul Newman's Hole in the Wall Camps. She recently finished a study on the effects of corporate philanthropy on leadership at Central Michigan

University. Currently Mary runs workshops, consults, and is an international speaker. She has also been a regular guest contributor to Global TV's *Money Wise, City TV,* and *CP24* on Canadian business issues.

Mary, welcome to *Stepping Stones to Success.*

Mary Donohue (Donohue)

Thank you very much, David.

Wright

So what is the biggest challenge facing corporations today?

Donohue

Trust is the biggest challenge that corporations face today, primarily because of the history of the last eight years. If you look at the headlines from 2000 to 2008, you will see how the leaders of corporations have chosen not to tell the truth, but have chosen to make sure that their key messages are what dominate the press. Politicians are no better. Think about the news stories about the Iraq war or Hurricane Katrina. Charities have also broken the trust—headlines inform us that charitable leaders have misappropriated funds. Through these key messages we have been preconditioned over the last nine years not to trust corporations, leaders, or charities.

The result of this clever key messaging that failed is that for the first time in more than 100 years, leaders are being thought of as villains before they are thought of as leaders. This response has been preconditioned by their actions and the headlines in the news. To rebuild trust, leaders have to give people a reason to trust them. They cannot assume that trust.

Wright

Will you explain what Leading by Giving™ is, and the benefits of using it to solve the problem?

Donohue

Leading by Giving is more than just engaging the follower to complete a task or to buy a product. Leading by Giving engages the whole person in an experience that demonstrates the value of the brand to a target audience, using corporate philanthropy. It moves philanthropy out of the one-dimensional telling stage—defined as telling consumers and staff how great the company is—to a multidimensional, experiential learning process that aligns the values of the brand with the values of the consumer.

Let me explain the difference between telling and providing an experience. Say your office has been invited to participate in a charity baseball tournament and you have been put in charge of getting the team ready. There is only one problem—no one in your office has ever played baseball. Do you just show your team a video, and then take them on to the field to play—no. Common sense tells you that wouldn't work. If you choose instead to take the time to prepare the team, holding a couple of practices and teaching them the rules of the game, everyone involved will have fun at the tournament and will have a higher opinion of you as a leader.

The problem with leadership today is that no one is taking that time to teach. Over the past forty years, our culture has progressively forced leaders into just telling people to play, and not taking the time to teach them how. Until the crash, CEOs and business people were all about short-term gain. Investing in people and corporations wasn't on the agenda; but short-term shareholder gain was.

Historian David McCullough said in the *Harvard Business Review* that we don't train leaders anymore. The current recession demonstrates what happens when you don't train leaders.

Leading by Giving is not a quick fix—it is a long-term investment that enables people to become aware of your business, your mission, vision, and values. It enables them to be satisfied that there is alignment between what you say and what you do. Leading by Giving provides opportunities for leaders to provide experiences that enable their audiences to believe and build value in their companies' brands. It takes a minimum of eight months before a change in trust and reputation will occur that is sustainable.

WRIGHT

What is moral purpose and would you explain its relationship to Leading by Giving?

DONOHUE

Moral purpose is the result of the experience that leaders provide. Moral purpose is the common denominator people use to differentiate a company from its competition. Moral purpose is the articulation of your mission and vision. It is the alignment between your actions and your communication.

An example of moral principles in action is Microsoft. Microsoft is a technology company. Their mission is to help people and businesses throughout the world realize their full potential. A member of the Royal Canadian Mounted Police in Toronto read Microsoft's mission and values and sent Bill Gates an e-mail in which he asked Mr. Gates to help his team create a program that would scan the Internet to capture people who use the Web to prey on kids. Believe it or not, Mr. Gates received the e-mail and he sent it to the president of Microsoft in Canada and the team began work on it. The new program that was developed without charge for the police has been an incredibly useful tool in helping officers track child predators.

Microsoft articulated moral purpose. They walked the talk.

WRIGHT

What are the key conditions for corporations to rebuild trust and how do the conditions relate to Leading by Giving?

DONOHUE

Leading by Giving articulates your moral purpose. Moral purpose reflects your culture. Could Microsoft have ordered its employees to volunteer to design this software free? No. Their culture had to support the idea of giving back for the project to work. The key conditions in understanding Leading by Giving relate to culture. Corporations should examine their beliefs, customs, rituals, ceremonies, and symbols.

Belief

Belief is how much people accept as true your mission vision and values. And right now, it is safe to say, no one believes in much, as our economy is clearly demonstrating. People are conditioned, through the actions of the last nine years, to believe that leaders and politicians lie. This is cause and effect. If you are driven only by your own personal goals, your decision matrix will be all about you and what you want. Why would people believe in your goals unless what you wanted aligned with what they needed and wanted?

People have no trust in corporations they feel have no moral compass. If you don't believe me, check out the textbook industry. I have been told that over and over again the editors make choices that suit their bottom line rather than that of the students. Why? Because if they reach the volume set by the CEO, they get their bonus. Is this wrong? Well, not if your moral purpose is only about you and your goals, but the publishing industry should not be surprised by the behavior that this encourages. Students understand how they are being manipulated and they find shortcuts to buying a book. They don't believe in the product, so they don't buy it.

Custom

An example of a corporate custom is corporate philanthropy. Almost all of the Fortune 500 companies give money to social causes. Yet many people, including their own staff, believe that this custom is for public relations purposes only. An April 2007 *McKinsey Quarterly* report indicated that globally, consumers and employees expect more from corporations than a perfunctory nod to giving. A 2007 McKinsey survey reported in *The New York Times* found that 68 percent of executives at large global corporations believe they made a positive contribution to the public good. However, in the United States, only 40 percent of consumers and employees agreed with this assessment and many do not believe that corporations make a difference. Sixty percent of the population doesn't believe that corporations are giving.

Another custom of corporations is advertising. Advertising often tells consumers about the moral purpose of a company. Yet when the custom of advertising doesn't align with the custom of giving, consumers detect a fraud. Say, for example, that through its philanthropy a restaurant supports non-violence against women, but its advertising shows women in skimpy tops and in compromising situations with men. What is the real message? The custom of giving doesn't match the vision for the brand articulated through the custom of advertising.

Leading by Giving enables leaders to question the alignment of their customs and the articulation of their vision of the brand.

Ritual

Rituals are practices that create culture. Rituals are how people experience your company's moral purpose. In the corporate world, the weekly status meeting is a ritual. Many leaders claim it is a time to brainstorm as a team about new business. Often at these meetings people are recognized for their work. Yet how many of you reading this have been in a weekly meeting and your leader is checking his or her BlackBerry, reading memos, and is clearly absorbed in his or her work and power? When it is required, he or she offers the perfect response and mouths the standard motivational leadership statements. The ritual of the weekly meeting run by a "BlackBerry bosses" instill in their staff an understanding that no matter what they do, there will always be something more important than their work. Is this motivating?

Never in a million years, did I think I would say this for publication, but sometimes I wish that there were still a lot of people who smoked, particularly leaders. When I first starting working, I had a boss named Michael MacDonald who smoked like a fiend. Mike steadily moved up in the company and his team was fiercely loyal to him. Why? Because the real conversations about business took place outside the building or in the "smoking area." He would talk with clients, the secretary (me), the typist, other division heads, anyone who was a smoker and was outside in that area at any time of day. Mike listened to people who were angry, stressed, happy, and even bored. The ritual of smoking enabled Mike to connect with lots of people in the company—the ones who smoked—and he absorbed what they said and learned from it. He then applied what he learned to his division, his team, and his career. Mike was really successful and a fantastic boss. We were all very loyal to him.

Leaders need to create rituals that connect with their staff, however, it should be an alternative to the smoking area idea.

Ceremonies

To rebuild this trust, corporations have to engage and educate and entice their employees, their consumers, and the media on the value of the corporation to their lives.

I interviewed one of the leaders of the Microsoft project I mentioned earlier, Paula Knight. Paula told me that the ceremony of supported corporate volunteering is the new rite of passage for leaders in the corporation. Paid volunteer work helps mid-level leaders find their voice and passion for the brand. Leaders who volunteer and are supported in this volunteering by their corporations become passionate about or believe in what the brand can do and what its leaders really believe. Ceremonies enable people to understand the rules of engagement in dealing with the corporation and its leaders.

Symbols

In my research with MolsonCoors Canada, we tested the effectiveness of volunteering on leadership development. The program is still in operation and is called The National Mentoring Program. With The National Mentoring Program™ (NMP), we created a number of signs that acknowledged volunteers at Molson, including awards and features on their work on the company Intranet. Volunteering at Molson, after all the analysis had been completed, emerged as a badge of honor for mid-level leaders and has become a basis for which other employees and consumers are able to judge the company. Volunteering in the community with students and with not-for-profits became a symbol of the brand and its commitment to communities in which Molson conducted business.

The research also outlined an interesting fact — the more the mid-level leaders engaged with others outside the community, the stronger they believed they became as a leader. The stronger their belief in themselves, the more they were willing to move up in the company, and believe in what the brand stood for, or believe in the culture of the company. They became loyal to the company.

The exact same sequence of events occurred for the students who were involved in the program — they began to believe in Molson and they became loyal to the brand. The symbol of The National Mentoring Program became anonymous with a brand that builds community and supports students and staff.

Symbols can also have a negative effect. Look at the current symbols of corporate leadership — too much artwork, a renovated office that costs millions of dollars, very expensive cars. What we're not seeing are the symbols of goodwill. We're not seeing the symbols of actual hard labor. What kind of a symbol is expressed in taking $50 million even when you're fired for doing a lousy job? People need to think about these things and about how they want to change them.

WRIGHT

What is the National Mentoring Program?

DONOHUE

The National Mentoring Program is an innovative sixteen-week mentorship and leadership-training program that links students, corporate leadership trainees, and nonprofit organizations in a unique partnership. Students apply for a position in the program. To apply, students must find a project at a nonprofit organization that fits with one of the sponsoring firm's giving priorities — either through the National Mentoring Program database, or through the firm's own. The database is created from applications nonprofits are invited to complete and through relationships with corporate partners that support the nonprofit organizations.

Applications are due in the early fall. Students must describe why they want to serve the nonprofit organization and the value that they would bring to the project. If a student's proposal is selected for the program, he or she would undertake the project at the nonprofit organization the following summer. The sponsoring corporation would donate to the nonprofit $7,000 to pay the salary of the student working to complete the project at the organization.

The truly differentiating factor of the NMP is that each student is assigned a mentor from the firm's management. The mentor works with the student and the nonprofit for sixteen weeks for twenty to thirty minutes a week through the winter and spring. The mentor provides advice on a number of fronts, including how to best complete the project and how to design and implement a strategic plan based on ethical leadership principles.

For example, in the past, a nonprofit organization needed help building its brand, the student was paired with someone from Molson who had experience in this area, subsequently increasing the volunteers and awareness of the program ten-fold at the end of the summer.

The NMP's overall goals are to improve employee satisfaction, develop leadership and mentorship skills for mid-level leaders, to help charities in need, and to provide funds to pay for school and invaluable work experience for university students.

WRIGHT

Would you describe the relationship of The National Mentoring Program with Leading by Giving?

DONOHUE

The National Mentoring Program was my dissertation research project and it tested the theory of Leading by Giving. The NMP enabled me to identify five stages of perception that consumers and staff alike go through when Leading by Giving is utilized. There are five stages: awareness, satisfaction, experience, believe, and value:

The 5 Stages of Perception

Awareness

Stage one occurs when the target audience becomes aware of the program. During the National Mentoring Program, employees and consumers became aware of Molson's philanthropic intent. This awareness of Molson and its desire to "help" was able to cut through the clutter of messages that people receive daily. The NMP increased the reach of Molson's message. Molson's philanthropic message cut through the clutter because it focused its message on how the NMP was going to help students, staff, and not-for-profits.

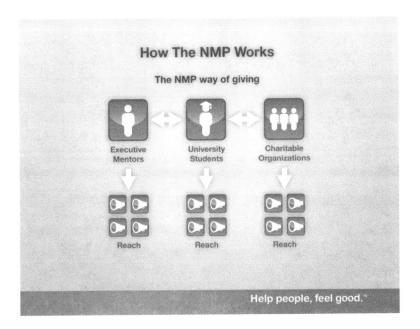

Satisfaction

The second stage is satisfaction. Consumers and staff alike have to be satisfied that the corporation is giving back, or that the corporation is doing what it said it was going to do. Consumers and staff have to be convinced that the organization (in this case Molson) is meeting the minimum standards in terms of philanthropy of corporate social responsibility. It is usually in this stage when consumer and staff perceive a false tone.

For example, when AIG gave the bonuses after they had received the TARP funding, people weren't satisfied it was meeting the basic criteria of what it agreed to when it took the money. AIG lost the perception of trust before anyone even had a chance to experience their brand.

Experience

The third stage, in terms of introspective leadership, is an experience. Leading by Giving requires that you create an experience that enables people to connect with the brand. This experience should help people feel good. It is while other people are helping community members that they change their opinions. What kind of experiences? For Microsoft it was the experience of using its talents to help police stop child sex predators. For Molson it was helping students earn money by working in a summer job while helping charities build business infrastructure.

Belief

The fourth stage is belief. Toward the final month of the NMP, the mid-level leaders reaffirmed their beliefs in themselves and in the corporation's ability to do good. The experiences associated with the program in the previous stage initiated a positive change in the students', charities', and mentors' perception of their abilities, the corporation's abilities, and the culture of the organization. This shift in belief facilitated an increased trust in the leadership of the corporation.

In the belief stage, people begin to share stories of their experience. They begin to talk to their friends and say, "You know what I did? I was able to help a student earn enough money to pay for university for a year." Many then told others about how Molson enabled a kid to stay in school and a charity to build infrastructure.

In my research, I actually identified that from seven people, one hundred and fifty-six heard the story firsthand. That's incredibly important. The figure below depicts the power of the belief stage. It shows how people communicate prior to Leading by Giving (old), and the new depicts what happens when people experience and subsequently believe in the brand. They tell two friends, who tell two friends, and so on.

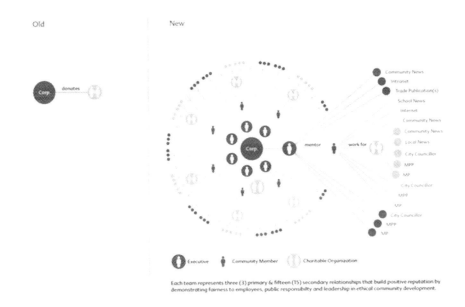

Old   New

Each team represents three (3) primary & fifteen (15) secondary relationships that build positive reputation by
demonstrating fairness to employees, public responsibility and leadership in ethical community development.

Value

After experiencing the brand and rebuilding trust in the brand, participants begin to see a value in their leader and the corporation associated with the leader. People begin to understand and become loyal. Once you create loyalty, you've begun to rebuild that trust.

What do you think happened to Molson when thirty-five students, thirty-five charities and thirty-five mentors began to talk to their friends about The National Mentoring Program? For research purposes, in year one, we compared the return on investment of funds invested in The National Mentoring Program with funds that were invested in a traditional not-for-profit gift. The results are below:

Giving Strategies	NMP investment of $50,000	
	Traditional Donation of $50,000	
Articulates values of Molson	✔	✔
Employee Involvement	✔	✔
Effects work satisfaction		✔
Effects career trajectory		✔
Effects leadership skills		✔
Effects internal perception of brand		✔
Effects leadership		✔
Effects intent to purchase		✔
Engages govt. officials		✔
National Media		✔
Magazine		✔
Community Media Hit	✔	✔
Charity Newsletter/Website	✔	✔
College Media		✔
FaceBook/Social Sites		✔
Blog (Online Coverage)		✔
TV		✔

©2008 Mary E. Donohue

WRIGHT

Would you define stage one, awareness, and perhaps the criteria to move on to stage two?

DONOHUE

Absolutely. In awareness, people become aware of the firm's commitment to developing its personal leadership skills and to developing an infrastructure for the communities in which they do business. If awareness is not present, the program will not move forward. Awareness is achieved by focusing on the needs of the target audience rather than the desire of the corporation. For example, Microsoft focused on the needs of the Royal Mounted Police rather than their desire for great press. Consumers know when programs are being run just to attract accolades.

In stage two, satisfaction, people are beginning to refine their previously held views of the brand. They begin to look through a new lens and they begin to see how the brand invested in them and how that investment may benefit them. Specifically, it enables employees to connect with consumers in the communities in which they conduct business.

What we find in the majority of people in the satisfaction stage is they have a tendency to want to believe in the good. Satisfaction is when people begin to be convinced that you are not lying about helping. They begin to see you walk the talk. When Bill Gates wrote in his mission statement, helping people and businesses realize their full potential, how many people really believed that was true? After reading in this section how Microsoft helped the police, do you (the reader) believe that the Microsoft really is determined to help people and business—I believe.

During the experience process, if you let people experience your brand and all it has to offer. The benchmark for success in the experience stage is *Help people, Feel good™*. If your program provides opportunities for learning and for growth, if you help people to improve, you are successful.

For example, let's go back to the Molson example and mentoring. In my Molson experiment, mentoring was the experience designed to *Help people, Feel good*. The mentors assisted young students in universities and not-for-profits who were hoping to increase their business infrastructure capacity. The mentors, for the first time in their working career, had to put down their BlackBerrys, step away from their computers, and actually talk to these young business students and charities about the issues that were facing them.

These experiences and conversations define for the participants the moral purpose of the company. Students and charities understood that Molson was proud to play a role in their education both as a mentor and a financial supporter. Molson's mission for their philanthropic endeavors is "Proud to Play our Part." Through the experience of The National Mentoring Program, students and employees experienced the moral purpose of the organization because mentors took the time to listen to what they needed rather than just decided as the expert what was needed. The mentors took pride in their role as mentor to the students and the not-for-profits.

Belief enables people to identify what is good and what works. It provides the content that consumers need to relate to the brand. During my research, one of my favorite quotes from the participants in the NMP was "I learned that Molson was willing to invest in the whole person, not just the person that bought beer but the person who needed to pay for school and the person who wanted to change the world." And because Leading by Giving offers consumers and staff this experience, they are able to say, "Wow! I believe more in this brand. I believe more in this company." Don't you think a parent whose university savings had been depleted by the crash would be saying that? Of course they would, and they did. Molson has kept almost fifty students using the NMP program alone from having to get a student loan and has provided almost fifty not-for-profits the opportunity to build their businesses.

WRIGHT

And would you define for our readers the last stage, value?

DONOHUE

The last stage is value. Value is when people feel good about experience of being connected to your brand. Right now we have a number of people who are feeling very bad about their jobs and about their community. We are seeing whole communities dying as we look at the auto industry.

Leading by Giving builds connections by creating experiences that utilize the strengths of corporations and their staffs to build community infrastructure. These experiences enable people to define and align with the moral purpose of the company. Through the experience, they compare the moral purpose of the company to their own beliefs. If the two align, they value the company for its contributions. When alignment occurs between the moral purpose of the firm and moral purpose of the consumer, trust is rebuilt and loyalty returns or increases.

WRIGHT

Why do you think Leading by Giving is such a great tool?

DONOHUE

In my research, and in the research of others, Leading by Giving has effected positive change. It is a system that builds community, culture, loyalty, and trust. Leading by Giving involves people in the brand rather than just asking them to be content to observe. Leading enables people to shine and use their talents to help others. It is fun and we all need a little fun in our lives.

WRIGHT

How does it affect staff, consumers, and the corporate culture?

DONOHUE

Earlier, I gave an example of how teaching baseball could enable people to see you as a strong leader. Leading by Giving is the same thing. It enables consumers to experience the brand and have fun with your corporation's staff and business experience. If people enjoy your brand they will be loyal to it.

Rather than tell people your brand is great, Leading by Giving allows them to experience it for themselves. Companies that have tried this leadership style have begun to shift their corporate cultures. It is too soon yet to see whether this corporate culture shift will be translated into our pop culture, but I am interested to see what happens when the leaders involved with The National Mentoring Program move up the ladder.

WRIGHT

Well what a great conversation, Mary. I really appreciate the time you've spent with me here this morning, answering all these questions. You've given me a lot to think about and I'm certainly going to look at these five steps as far as my own company is concerned.

DONOHUE

Thank you.

WRIGHT

We have been talking with Dr. Mary Donohue, a management analyst. She has a unique ability to create a sense of excitement and fun about her initiatives, motivating her clients and their customers to get fully engaged. After hearing her here this morning, I understand why executives and clients refer to her as a fireball and an idea tornado.

Mary, thank you so much for being with us today on *Stepping Stones to Success*.

DONOHUE

Thank you, David.

ABOUT THE AUTHOR

Today we're talking with Mary Donohue, EdD. She an author, journalist and founder of the National Mentoring Program. Mary has worked in New York, San Francisco, and Toronto. She boasts a history of public relations, event planning, operations, and management as shown by rapid sales growth and advancement with such companies as MolsonCoors Canada (Molson), Red Bull, Honda, and Nike. Dr. Mary has a unique ability to create a sense of excitement and fun about her initiatives, motivating her clients and their customers to get fully engaged. She was described at a recent press conference by Paul Godfrey, former president of the Toronto Blue Jays Baseball Club, as a fireball and has been described by others as an idea tornado.

While learning about great leaders and ethics, Mary met and was moved to innovation by Paul Newman. Subsequently she completed her internship for her doctorate with Paul Newman's Hole in the Wall Camps. She recently finished a study on the effects of corporate philanthropy on leadership at Central Michigan University. Currently Mary runs workshops, consults, and is an international speaker. She has also been a regular guest contributor to Global TV's *Money Wise, City TV*, and *CP24* on Canadian business issues.

DR. MARY DONOHUE, EdD

1 First Canadian Place
Suite 350
Toronto ON M5X 1C1
416 915 3182 office
416 564 2944 cell
mary@thenmp.com
www.thenmp.com

CHAPTER NINE

Develop a Disciplined Life

AN INTERVIEW WITH.... DR. DENIS WAITLEY

DAVID WRIGHT (WRIGHT)

Today we are talking with Dr. Denis Waitley. Denis is one of America's most respected authors, keynote lecturers, and productivity consultants on high performance human achievement. He has inspired, informed, challenged, and entertained audiences for more than twenty-five years from the boardrooms of multi-national corporations to the control rooms of NASA's space program and from the locker rooms of world-class athletes to the meeting rooms of thousands of conventioneers throughout the world.

With more than ten million audio programs sold in fourteen languages, Denis Waitley is the most listened-to voice on personal and career success. He is the author of twelve non-fiction books, including several international bestsellers. His audio album, "The Psychology of Winning," is the all-time best-selling program on self-mastery. Dr. Waitley is a founding director of the National Council on Self-Esteem and the President's Council on Vocational Education. He recently received the "Youth Flame Award" from the National Council on Youth Leadership for his outstanding contribution to high school youth leadership.

A graduate of the U.S. Naval Academy Annapolis, and former Navy pilot, he holds a doctorate degree in human behavior.

Denis, it is my sincere pleasure to welcome you to *Stepping Stones to Success!* Thank you for being with us today.

DENIS WAITLEY (WAITLEY)

David, it's great to be with you again. It's been too long. I always get excited when I know you're going to call. Maybe we can make some good things happen for those who are really interested in getting ahead and moving forward with their own careers in their lives.

WRIGHT

I know our readers would enjoy hearing you talk about your formative years. Will you tell us a little about your life growing up in the context of what you've achieved and what shaped you into the person you are today? Do you remember one or two pivotal experiences that propelled you on the path you eventually chose?

WAITLEY

I believe many of us are redwood trees in a flowerpot. We've become root-bound by our earlier environment and it's up to each of us to realize that and break out of our flower pot if we're going to grow to our full potential.

I remember my father left our home when I was a little boy. He said goodnight and goodbye and suddenly I became the man of the family at age nine. My little brother was only two, so I had to carry him around as my little shadow for the ensuing years. To this day my kid brother has always looked at me as his dad, even though there is only seven years' difference between us. He'll phone me and ask what he should do and I'll tell him, "I'm your brother, not your father!"

Our dad was a great guy but he drank too much and had some habits that took a firm hold on him. He never abused me and always expected more from me than he did from himself. I had a push-pull—on the one hand, I felt inadequate and guilty when I would go to succeed but on the other hand, Dad kept feeding me the idea that he missed his ship and I'd catch mine. The only thing I could do to get out of that roller coaster impact was to ride my bicycle twenty miles every Saturday over to my grandmother's house. She was my escape. I would mow her lawn and she would give me such great feedback and reinforcement. She told me to plant the seeds of greatness as she and I planted our "victory garden" during World War II. She told me that weeds would come unannounced and uninvited—I didn't need to worry about weeds coming into my life, they didn't even need to be watered.

I said, "Wow! You don't have to water weeds?"

"No," she replied, "they'll show up in your life and what you need to do, my grandson, is model your life after people who've been consistent and real in their contribution as role models and mentors."

She also told me that a library card would eventually be much more valuable than a Master Card. Because of my grandmother reading biographies of people who'd overcome so much more than I was going through, I thought, "Wow! I don't have any problems compared to some of these great people in history who really came from behind to get ahead." I think that was my start in life.

I went to the Naval Academy because the Korean War was in force and you had to serve your country, so the best way was to run and hide in an academy. If you earned enough good grades you were put through without a scholarship or without money from your parents. Since my parents didn't have any money, it was a great way to get a college education.

I became a Navy pilot after that and learned that if you simulate and rehearse properly you'll probably learn to fly that machine. But much of it has to do with the amount of practice you put into ground school and into going through the paces. As I gained experience being a Navy pilot, I eventually decided to go on and get my advanced degree in psychology because I wanted to develop people rather than stay in the military. I pursued a program where I could take my military and more disciplined background and put it into human development. That's basically the story.

I earned my doctorate, I met Jonas Salk, and Dr. Salk introduced me to some pioneers in the behavioral field. Then along came Earl Nightingale who heard just a simple taped evening speech of mine and decided that maybe my voice was good enough, even though I was a "new kid on the block," to maybe do an album on personal development, which I did in 1978. It surprised me the most, and everyone else also, that it became one of the bestsellers of all time.

WRIGHT

Being a graduate of Annapolis and having been a Navy pilot, to what degree did your experience in the Navy shape your life and your ideas about productivity and performance?

WAITLEY

David, I think those experiences shaped my life and ideas a great deal. I was an original surfer boy from California and when I entered the Naval Academy I found that surfer boys had their heads shaved and were told to go stand in line—everyone's successful so you're nothing special. I found myself on a team that was very competitive but at the same time had good camaraderie.

I realized that I didn't have the kind of discipline structure in my life that I needed. I also discovered that all these other guys were as talented, or more talented, than I was. What that shaped for me was realizing that the effort required to become successful is habit-forming. I think I learned healthy habits at the Academy and as a Navy pilot just to stay alive. To perform these kinds of functions I really had to have a more disciplined life. That set me on my stage for working more on a daily basis at habit formation than just being a positive thinker only.

WRIGHT

In our book, *Stepping Stones to Success,* we're exploring a variety of issues related to human nature and the quest to succeed. In your best-selling program, *The Psychology of Winning,* you focus on building self-esteem, motivation, and self-discipline. Why are these so crucial to winning and success?

WAITLEY

They're so crucial they're misunderstood. I think especially the term "self-esteem" is misunderstood. We've spent a fortune and we had a California committee on it—we formed the National Council on Self-Esteem. What has happened, in my opinion, is that self-esteem has been misused and misjudged as being self-indulgence, self-gratification—a celebrity kind of mentality. We've put too much emphasis on the wrong idea about self-esteem.

Self-esteem is actually the deep down, inside the skin feeling of your own worth regardless of your age, ethnicity, gender, or level of current performance. It's really a belief that you're good enough to invest in education and effort and you believe some kind of dream when that's all you have to hang onto.

What's happened, unfortunately, is that we've paid so much attention to self-esteem it's become a celebrity and an arena mentality kind of concept. Most people are "struttin' their stuff" and they're celebrating after every good play on the athletic field, whereas, if you're a *real* professional, that's what you do anyway. A real professional is humble, gracious, and understands fans. I think that what we've done is put too much emphasis on asserting one's self and believing that you're the greatest and then talking about it too much or showing off too much in order to make that self-esteem public.

The real self-esteem has two aspects: 1) Believing that you deserve as much as anyone else and that you're worthy. Someone may look at you and tell you they see real potential in you. If you can feel that you have potential and you're worth the effort, that's the first step. 2) The second step is to start doing things to give you confidence so that when you do something and learn something it works out and you'll get the self-confidence that comes from reinforcing small successes. That combination of expectation and reinforcement is fundamental to anyone who wants to be a high achiever. That's what self-esteem is really all about—deserving on the one hand and reinforcing success in small ways to get your motor running and feel the confidence that you can do better than you have been.

Fears crop up and get in the way of our motivation. In my case I was afraid of success. Nobody had ever succeeded in our family and because they hadn't, I felt inadequate to be able to succeed. Whenever it would show up around the corner I would think, "Well, this is too good to be true for me—I don't deserve that." So I would feel a little bit doubtful of my abilities. When I would succeed, there would be an attendant, "Yelp!" I would feel because I would not believe I deserved what I had achieved.

I think fear is the thing that gets in the way of our motivation because we're all motivated by inhibitions and compulsions. You should be motivated more by the result you want rather than the penalty. That's why I've always said that winners are motivated by reward of success rather than inhibited or compelled by the penalty of failure. If you get this conviction that you're as good as the best but no better than the rest—I'm worth the effort, I'm not Mr. Wonderful, I'm not the center of the universe but I can do some things that I haven't done yet—and then apply this motivation to desire rather than fear, that is when self-discipline comes into play.

I'd have to say, David, I could spend the entire interview on self-discipline because I missed it as one of the most important ingredients in success. I've always been a belief guy, an optimism guy, a faith guy, and all the self-esteem things but I think, as time went on, I forgot the amount of discipline it takes for anyone who is a champion in any endeavor. I think I'm back on that track now.

WRIGHT

I can really appreciate the Flame Award you won from the National Council on Youth Leadership for helping high school leaders. I've got a daughter in college and I know how difficult and important it is. But in some circles, self-esteem has gotten a bad reputation. For example, in many schools, teachers won't reward high achievers for fear of hurting the self-esteem of others in the classroom. Many people feel this is not helpful to these children.

In your opinion, where is the balance between building healthy self-esteem and preparing kids and adults to cope and succeed in a competitive world?

WAITLEY

I think that there has to first of all be some kind of performance standard. A good example is the Olympic Games. The idea of the Olympic Games is to set a standard that you've tried to live up to in your own way as a world-class person, realizing that there can only be so many Olympians and so many gold medalists and so on. I think, on the one hand, it's really important to have standards because if you have a standard, then you have something tangible to shoot for or to measure against.

I think there's a problem, however, in that only so many people can be medalists and win medals at the Olympics. One of the reasons that the high jump bar, for example, is set so that everyone can jump over it the first time, is to experience the feeling of success that first jump produces. The feeling of success is working in the competitor before the bar is raised to world record height and to much higher standards than even the normal Olympian.

I'm one who believes in testing. It's difficult when you have a "No Child Left Behind" concept because many times today we're going pass/fail. We're moving people up through the grades regardless of their performance simply because we don't want them left behind and therefore feeling that they're not able to function simply because they can't compete with some students who've been given many more opportunities to succeed than others.

Having said that, I'd say that healthy self-esteem is gained by giving specific stair-step, incremental, bite-sized pieces; perhaps there needs to be several different standards set. Usually the grading system does that and the point system does that where you have someone who has a four point three grade average because of all the extra credits they're taking. Then you have those with a three point eight and then those who are just barely passing. Unfortunately then, what that does is enable only a few people to get into universities and the others have to go to community colleges.

What I will have to say, however, is that we in the United States have to be very careful that we don't dumb down or lower our standards for excellence in our schools. Traveling as much as I do, I have discovered information about this. For example, there are 300 universities in Beijing alone—just in one city in China. The way it goes internationally is that the public schools in Japan, for example, are much more competitive than the private schools. If you're in Japan going to a public school, you have to really perform up to the highest standards in order to ever think of qualifying for any kind of university. You'd have to go into a vocational school if you didn't compete in higher standards in public schools in Japan. The same thing is true in Singapore, China, and in the developing nations.

We have a situation brewing here where we've got global developing countries with really high standards in English, mathematics, engineering, and science. And we have educators in the United States who are more concerned about making sure that the self-esteem of an individual doesn't get damaged by this competitive standard. I think we have to maintain standards of excellence.

I wish we had kept dress codes in schools. I have found schools that have marching bands. A certain amount of uniformity not only encourages greater athletic performance but higher academic standards as well. The same is true globally. There's an argument that if you put kids in uniforms, you're going to limit their creative thinking. The truth is, if you can standardize the way people appear in their style, then you can focus more on substance—their experience, imagination, contribution, and their study. The core of an individual rather than the surface of an individual can be developed much better. It would be great if we could combine the more disciplined aspects of the developing countries with the more entrepreneurial, creative, free-thinking aspects of our society, which means we're critical thinkers (i.e., you throw us a problem and we'll try everything we can possibly think of to solve it). In the developing countries they'll use a textbook or an older person's experience rather than using critical thinking.

We're very entrepreneurial here in America, but I'm very much concerned that our standards are being lowered too much. If we're not careful, we're going to take our place in the future as a second-rate educational country and therefore forfeit the idea of being a technological and market leader.

WRIGHT

I also hear grumbling about motivation. I'm sure you've seen business people roll their eyes a bit at the mention of listening to "motivational" tapes or CDs. Some tire of getting all hyped up about change or sales goals, for example, only to lose their excitement and fail to reach their goals. Are they missing something critical about the nature or application of motivation?

WAITLEY

I really believe they are, David. I think they're missing the idea that what you *want* in life turns you on much more than what you *need* in life. Too often business managers even today focus on the hard skills because they say that the other skills are "soft skills." Well, there's no such thing as a hard or soft skill because you can't separate your personal from your professional life anymore. You get fired more for personal reasons—for being late, for your habits, for you hygiene, your behavior, your anger. This idea that technical training as opposed to motivation is the way to go is misguided.

I have found that employees are excited and are full of desire and energy because management listens to them, reinforces them, is interested in their personal goals, and is interested in keeping them inspired. That inspiration is what we remember. So, when we go to a meeting we remember how we felt about the meeting, not the specifics of the meeting.

I think this emotional component—keeping people's energy and desires foremost and doing a desire analysis of employees rather than just a needs analysis—is very, very important. I often think this is lost in the idea that we're giving a pep talk, or a quick fix, or a Band-Aid when, as Zig Ziglar has mentioned so many times, "Motivation is like taking a bath. You take a bath every day and you might say why take a bath—you're going to get dirty anyway." But the very nature of doing it, and doing it on a habitual basis, makes this positive energy continue to flow and motivation becomes habit-forming. I think you need a lot of it to keep these habits of excellence or else you'll just be running scared—you'll be afraid not to do well because you'll lose your job.

Believe it or not, we have a lot of employees in America who are working harder than they ever have before so they won't be fired. That's not really the way to go after a goal—constantly looking through the rear view mirror trying to cover your behind.

WRIGHT

If you don't mind, I'd like to change the focus a little to the topic of self-discipline. People seem to know what they should do and how they should change, but they just can't discipline themselves to take the necessary steps to do so. What is the secret to becoming a disciplined person?

WAITLEY

I think the secret is to get a team, a support group, a mastermind group because not only is there safety in numbers but there's accountability in numbers. When we are accountable to one another to maintain a certain standard of discipline, it's much easier to work out if someone else is getting up at six-thirty in the morning with you. It's much easier to have a support group if you're interested in maintaining a healthier diet, for example, because the temptations are irresistible to procrastinate and to fall off the wagon. That's why I believe you need a team effort.

It also has to be understood in an immediate gratification society that there is no "success pill" that you can swallow. There is no quick way to get rich and get to the top. There is this steady ratcheting to the top and that's why I think leaders need to say it's going to take us about a year to get any permanent change going. So, I think we should all understand there may be a little dip in productivity as we start this new program of ours—a little dip at first and a little uncertainty—but over time, over about a year, we're going to become like an astronaut or an Olympian. We need to engrain these ideas so they become reflexive. It takes about a year for an idea or a habit to become a reflex. This idea of being able to do it in twenty-one days is misguided. I don't think it takes twenty-one days to learn a skill. It may take twenty-one days to learn to type, it may take twenty-one days to begin to learn a skill, but it takes a year for it to get into the subconscious and take hold.

I think we have to learn that discipline is practicing on a daily basis for about a year so that it will become a habit—a pattern—that will override the old inner software program.

WRIGHT

I'm a big believer in the greater potential of the individual. I remember a fellow—Paul Myer—who helped me a lot when I was a young guy. He was in Waco, Texas, with a company called Success Motivation Institute. You may know him.

WAITLEY

I know him very well. Actually, he's one of the icons and pioneers in this entire field. He and Earl Nightingale were the first ones to ever have a recorded speaking message other than music. Earl and Paul were pioneers in audio recording and I have still a great respect for Paul. I spoke for his organization some time ago.

WRIGHT

He personally helped me a lot when I was younger and I just really appreciated him. In your book and program, *Seeds of Greatness*, you outline a system for nurturing greatness. Will you give us a brief overview of this program?

WAITLEY

It's taken me thirty years to get this thing to where I want it. I wrote the book twenty years ago titled, *Seeds of Greatness,* and sure, it became a bestseller but so did *One Minute Manager, In Search of Excellence, Iacocca,* and every other book at that time. I have trouble keeping that thing pumped up.

Over the years I've found that *Seeds of Greatness,* for me, has been a system. What I've had to do is go back through all the mistakes I've made as a family leader. I knew I was a father and not a mother *and* father so I had to find a mother who was also a good clinical psychologist and who had worked with every form of behavioral problem. We put our efforts together so that we had a man and a woman as family leaders with clinical and other experience who could give parents or leaders of the day a certain track to run on where they could coach their small children and adolescents on a daily basis.

I provided a perpetual calendar that gives coaching tips of the day—what I call "sign on the day" and "sign off the day"—for parents to use to communicate with their kids. Then I had to put nineteen CDs together—audio tracks—that covered these "roots and wings," which I would call the "core values" and the more motivational or, if you will, ways to set your kids free.

The idea of parenthood should be to lay the groundwork, make it safe to fail an experiment, and then send them off on their own as independent, not codependent, young adults so they can reach their own destiny. I divided it into "roots of core values" and "wings of self-motivation and self-direction" and tried to balance the two so that whether you're from a blended family, or a single parent family, and whether you're structurally religious or whether you're spiritually religious, it would work, regardless of your personal core belief system.

I'm very happy that we've finally put together a self-study program that can be taught by the authors or by people who are licensed facilitators. It's something that a family leadership group could take and work on their own at their own speed by watching, listening, interacting with their kids, and using a combination of a written book, the audios, the DVDs, and this coaching calendar to maybe put it all together so that over a period of six months to a year they might be able to effect some changes in the way they interact with their kids.

WRIGHT

Sounds great! Before our time runs out, would you share a story or two about your real life coaching and consulting experiences? I know you've coached astronauts and Super Bowl champions as well, haven't you?

WAITLEY

Well, I have. I've been lucky to work within the Apollo program in the simulation area. I found that simulation prevents failure of the first attempt. In other words, if you're going to go to the moon and they're going to shoot you up a quarter of a million miles up and back in a government vehicle, you had better have your rehearsal down and really pat. The astronauts teach you that the dress rehearsal is life or death. The Olympians teach you that at the moment you go to perform, you need to clear your mind so you can remember everything you learned without trying—you develop muscle memory and reflex.

Twenty-one years ago when Mary Lou Retton was doing the vault, she needed a nine point nine five to tie the Romanian for the gold medal in women's all around gymnastics. I asked her what she was thinking about when she went to vault and she said, "Oh gosh, I guess what everyone thinks about—speed, power, explode, extend, rotate, plant your feet at the end. When the pressure is on I get better just like drill. 'Come on, Mary Lou, this is your moment in history!' "

I thought, "Wow! That's not what everyone thinks. What everyone thinks is, 'Thank God it's Friday,' 'Why me?' 'Don't work too hard,' 'Countin' down to Friday,' 'Looking to five P.M.,' 'Romanians are better trained, probably on steroids,' " So I get these stories of Olympians who have internalized this wonderful running the race in advance and simulating as well.

I guess the one story that I'll share is about a ten-year-old boy. In about 1980 this boy came to a goal-setting seminar. He told me that none of the people who had paid their money were really working on their goals. They were really thinking about what they were going to eat and golf. I gave him a work book and told him to go back and do what they were supposed to do and write down his abilities and liabilities, what he was going to do this year and next year and five years from now and twenty years from now. He got all excited because he thought it was this wonderful game that you can play called, Write the Future, or Describe the Future.

So he ran back and worked on the project and forty-five minutes later he astounded the adults in the audience by saying he was earning money mowing lawns and shoveling snow so he could go to Hawaii on the fourteenth of July to snorkel on the big island of Hawaii's Kona Coast. Then he said next year he'd be eleven going into the fifth grade and he was going to build models of what was going to be a space shuttle and he was going to begin to learn more about numbers and math. In five years he'd be fifteen and as a tenth-grader. He said he would study math and science because he wanted to go to the Air Force academy—he was all excited about that. I asked him what he was going to be doing in twenty years and he said he'd be an astronaut delivering UPS packages in space.

I forgot all about him and twenty years later, sure enough, I saw him on the *Today Show* as they showed a picture of an astronaut on a tether line pulling the satellite into the bay of the space shuttle. I thought, "My gosh! This kid did what I only talk about in the seminars." He was a living, breathing example of someone who was focused on this. I said to my family, "Look at what he did!" And they said, "What have *you* been doing for the last twenty years?" I said I was a goal tender. They told me I should be a goal achiever too.

WRIGHT

What a great conversation. I always enjoy talking with you. It's not just uplifting—I always learn a lot when I talk with you.

WAITLEY

Well, David, I do with you as well. You've got a great program and you do a lot of good for people who read and watch and listen. I think you give them insights that otherwise they would never get. I'm just grateful to be one of the contributors and one of the members of your global team.

WRIGHT

It has been my sincere pleasure today to visit with a truly great American, Dr. Denis Waitley.

Denis, thank you for taking so much of your time to share your insights and inspirations for us here on *Stepping Stones to Success*.

WAITLEY

Thank you very much, David.

DENIS WAITLEY is one of America's most respected authors, keynote lecturers and productivity consultants on high performance human achievement. He has inspired, informed, challenged, and entertained audiences for over twenty-five years from the board rooms of multi-national corporations to the control rooms of NASA's space program and from the locker rooms of world-class athletes to the meeting rooms of thousands of conventioneers throughout the world. He was voted business speaker of the year by the Sales and Marketing Executives Association and by Toastmasters International and inducted into the International Speakers Hall of Fame. With over ten million audio programs sold in fourteen languages, Denis Waitley is the most listened-to voice on personal and career success. He is the author of twelve non-fiction books, including several international bestsellers, *Seeds of Greatness, Being the Best, The Winner's Edge, The Joy of Working*, and *Empires of the Mind*. His audio album, "The Psychology of Winning," is the all-time best-selling program on self-mastery.

DR. DENIS WAITLEY
The Waitley Institute
P.O. Box 197
Rancho Santa Fe, CA 92067
www.deniswaitley.com

CHAPTER TEN

Is Network Marketing & Direct Sales the Future in this Economy?

DAVID WRIGHT (WRIGHT)

Today we're talking with Cedrick Harris. He is an internationally recognized trainer, speaker, and author in the network marketing and direct sales industry. In 2006, after spending some very successful years in the mortgage industry as the president of marketing for a very large mortgage company, Cedrick decided to share his knowledge of the Internet with fellow entrepreneurs worldwide. His passion for direct sales and network marketing moved him to start Team Takeover Marketing LLC, a sales and marketing company focused on teaching entrepreneurs how to take over their lives both mentally and financially in the home-based business arena. His company has grown to over two thousand members worldwide, and Cedrick prides himself on teaching his philosophies on Internet marketing, closing skills, prospecting, and network marketing. He is considered one of the hottest rising superstars in the direct sales and in the network marketing arena.

Cedrick Harris, welcome to *Stepping Stones for Success.*

CEDRICK HARRIS (HARRIS)

Thank you David, I'm excited to be here. It is my pleasure to be sharing this time with you here today.

WRIGHT

So you started your direct sales career as a teenager, but how did you get into the industry so young?

HARRIS

Well, David, my direct sales career started out very interesting. I was a freshman in high school and noticed one of my friends making a lucrative living selling candy to students. Growing up with a father who was an entrepreneur, I was immediately attracted to making money. So I went to my father and asked him to purchase some Blow Pops, Reese's Cups, and Now and Laters.

After a few weeks, I was actually making around eighty dollars per day selling candy as a teenager. As a fifteen-year-old kid, this was a lot of money to me. I still remember the day my mother came home one day and saw me counting my money. She immediately asked me, "Cedrick, how did you make that much money at school?" When I told her it was from selling candy, she laughed and made a statement that changed my life forever. She said, "Well, if you can make eighty dollars a day selling candy, you don't need me to buy you anymore school clothes or sneakers anymore." From that point forward I was responsible for making my own money for whatever I wanted in life. This was the best lesson my mother ever taught me and it launched my sales career into what it is today.

WRIGHT

So what attracted you to network marketing?

HARRIS

Network marketing was something that I actually came across by accident. In the early 1990s I was a manager for a food company called American Frozen Foods. I had eight sales reps who were responsible for selling a food service to residential customers in Richmond, Virginia. One day, one of my top reps, Todd, came to me and said one of his customers tried to recruit him into a network marketing company that looked pretty good.

At this point I didn't even know what network marketing was, so I decided to call his customer and ask him about the company. The company happened to be a long-distance company called Excel Communications. (This was after the deregulation of all of the major phone companies.) This posed a lucrative opportunity in the communications arena and I immediately saw the vision and the power of network marketing. Having been in sales for a few years, once I saw how a network marketer was paid, I was immediately sold. The concept of 1 percent of one hundred people is better than 100 percent of yourself. That was the concept that kept me up late at night focusing on perfecting my craft in this industry.

WRIGHT

How did you become so passionate about sales and network marketing?

HARRIS

My passion about sales and network marketing skyrocketed after a certain incident in my life changed everything. David, when I was eighteen years old, fresh out of high school, I had a lot of time on my hands. I really wasn't interested in going to college so I worked as a salesman at a clothing store called Cavalier Men's Shop in Richmond, Virginia.

One of my best friends I grew up with was a "pharmaceutical salesman" and he was making a lot of money doing this. Being attracted to fast money, I decided to join him and started to make a lot of money selling "illegal pharmaceuticals." Well, that pharmaceutical sales career didn't last very long, as I was arrested in 1993 and sent to a ninety-day boot camp program. This was the toughest thing I ever had to endure up to this point in my life and it was a very hard and humbling experience.

After completing boot camp I was able to come home knowing that I could accomplish anything in life because I had survived that crazy place. However, due to my record, the average employer wouldn't give me a chance to prove myself.

Still possessing some great sales skills, I finally landed a job in sales again and started moving up the economic ladder. Due to my earlier challenges, when I found out that it didn't matter what your background was when it came to network marketing, I was even more excited. I was tired of people prejudging me because of my past; in network marketing I never had to worry about that. My past actually fueled me to empower others to pursue direct sales and network marketing because you are able to write your own ticket. No longer do you have to worry about your past—just focus on the present and who you are becoming and life will throw you quite a few home runs.

WRIGHT

Would you give us a couple of examples of people who have played the largest part and had the biggest influence in your direct sales and network marketing career?

HARRIS

Well, in my direct sales career, David, that would have to be Bill Edwards. He is the owner of the largest veterans mortgage lender in the country, Mortgage Investors Corporation. Back in 2001, I answered an ad in the *Richmond Times Dispatch* that read, "This will be the last job you will ever have!" Being that the ad was so bold, I had to respond.

I interviewed for a loan officer position doing refinances for Mortgage Investors and was hired on the spot. Within ninety days I was the number two loan officer in the whole company out of over five hundred loan officers in twenty-eight different states.

After being promoted to manager and running the largest, most successful office in the company's sixty-three-year history, Bill offered me a position as the Senior Vice President of Marketing for the whole company. This was a great accomplishment, as I was able to move to Florida, run the company, and be mentored and coached on a daily basis by a multimillionaire. This was an invaluable lesson; I couldn't have asked for a better mentor to learn from in the mortgage and sales industry.

Bill is a seasoned veteran in sales and he taught me so many things that I still apply in my sales career—and life for that matter. He didn't care about my background because his focus was on results. I learned from him that truly the only thing that matters is results. People talk a good game a lot, but without results none of that means anything. Being mentored by Bill for so many years, I was able to see and accomplish things that I never thought possible.

Because of Bill, I was able to make a significant income in the mortgage industry starting at a very young age, and for that I am forever grateful for his mentorship and caring heart.

Within my network marketing career, the person who has had the biggest influence on me would have to be my coach and mentor, Jeffery Combs. Jeffery Combs is the President and Founder of Golden Mastermind Seminars, Inc, President of More Heart than Talent Publishing, a public speaker, published author, and mentor to thousands in this industry. I started studying Jeffery's material in 2005 while I was still in the mortgage industry. I was intrigued by his delivery, knowledge, and passion for getting results out of life.

Once I left the mortgage industry in 2006, I started to attend numerous seminars and workshops for direct sales and network marketing. I was able to see Jeffery at a few of these events but I was never able to speak to him directly. Then in January of 2008 I attended his "More Heart than Talent" workshop held in Texas every year. This event changed my life forever, as I knew I had to get to know Jeffery better because I wanted to share the stage with him in a public speaking environment. At that event I purchased all of Jeffery's material and started studying and practicing everything he taught.

A few months later, Jeffery held an event in my hometown of Florida where I was able to spend some quality one-on-one time with him. Within this time, I hired Jeffery as my personal coach and mentor. Since then he has helped me with numerous breakthroughs in my life. He has introduced me to some very influential people, he helped me with my very first CD series, he has been very influential in my public speaking career, and he was also very instrumental in the success of my network marketing career. Jeffery is someone I can truly say I love. He has had a great influence on the direction of my life.

WRIGHT

What three things have been your foundational steppingstones for success?

HARRIS

My first foundational steppingstone for success would have to be focus. I have learned that whatever you focus on in life you will get, period. When I was young, my focus was on fast money, so I got it. I also received the consequences of focusing on fast money.

Once I acquired more wisdom, I started channeling my energy on things that I wanted out of life. I started attending numerous sales and networking seminars. I started studying the people I wanted to be like. I surrounded myself with successful people who had what I wanted, not what I already had. Since that time my focus has paid off in *huge* dividends. Due to that focus, I have landed numerous public speaking engagements, have affected thousands of people's lives in this industry, and I am recognized as a top authority in the home based business arena.

Without true focus and a vision, none of these things would be possible. Most people really don't understand how powerful focus is in their lives. Most people focus on the wrong things and wonder why they get them not knowing that whatever you focus on you will receive, period.

With that being said, I recommend that you focus on abundance. Focus on becoming a better person. Focus on becoming someone who affects the masses. Focus on having a positive outlook about life. Focus of what you want, not what you don't want and watch how your life changes right in front of your very eyes.

My second foundational steppingstone to success would be listening to people who have what you want instead of people who have what you already have. This is a concept that has truly changed my life forever. When I was growing up as a teenager, the people who had what I wanted were not good role models. However, I listened to them because they had what I wanted — fast money, women, cars, and clothes. By listening to them, I was also able to see those luxuries too — before getting caught just like they were!

Then, when I got my focus right, I started listening to people like Bill Edwards, Jeffery Combs, Jim Rohn, Zig Ziglar, Brian Tracy, Mark Victor Hansen, Russell Simmons, and Og Mandino. I started to receive the same results they had early in their careers.

I learned from Og Mandino many years ago that "energy flows where attention goes." By focusing your energy on the things you want out of life, you will give it more attention. This attention will manifest into action, which will ultimately manifest into the result you were looking to acquire. Surrounding yourself around great people will only enhance your odds of greatness. If you know that you will ultimately become like the top five people you spend the most time with, isn't it smart to pick these people wisely?

Consider these facts:

- If you spend your time with millionaires, your chances of becoming one will be increased dramatically. If you spend your time with successful businesspeople, your chances of becoming one will be increased dramatically.
- If you spend your time with unsuccessful people, your chances of becoming one will be increased dramatically.

If you know these facts, doesn't it just make sense to listen to people who have what you want instead of people who have what you already have?

Last but not least, my third steppingstone for success would have to be persistence. I've had a lot of challenges growing up in my life where many people told me I couldn't do certain things because of my attitude and focus. However, having a certain drive determines everything. The persistence you have to prove the naysayers wrong has to burn. Your persistence to take care of your family, no matter what, has to drive you. Your persistence to keep getting rejected until you get that one yes has to burn in your gut.

Persistence can't be purchased; you have to own it inside of you, period. You have to be Sylvester Stallone in a Rocky movie—just keep getting up. Every time you get knocked down you have to get back up. If you are persistent enough, you will accomplish *anything* that you want in life no matter what. No excuses overcome the word persistence—*no excuses.*

David, those would be my three steppingstones for success, my friend.

WRIGHT

Many people define success differently. What is your definition of success?

HARRIS

My definition of success, David, is being successful spiritually and mentally, as well as financially. A lot of people define success by the size of one's bank account and I tend to disagree. I feel success first starts mentally. You must feel successful on the inside before you will see any results on the outside. This will take some serious soul-searching. This is where you will really need to decide the direction you want in life. This is the point when you may have to eliminate some people from your life who really don't serve a good purpose to you. This is where you really start to study the people you want to emulate. Accomplishing this step is a very important part of your having true success.

Once I started applying this in my life, I can truly say everything changed for the better. This decision may even be one of the hardest decisions in your life; however, it is so well worth it.

Secondly, I feel you have to be in touch with your spiritual side also. No matter who your deity is, you must understand that there is a force greater than you controlling the universe. When you're in touch with your deity, this will give you a certain inner peace that you're on the right path. You will ultimately know when you're in touch with your inner deity, because you will feel it. This is something that is hard to explain, but there is a certain feeling you will have as a human when you're in the flow spiritually.

Trying to be successful in life in general without getting in touch with your spiritual side will be empty. There is no success without God, period. Getting in touch with your spiritual side is a necessity like air, if you really want to be successful in whatever you do.

WRIGHT

You've had all this experience in the direct sales and network marketing arena for most of your life, what do you think are some key components you consider when looking at a business venture?

HARRIS

The first would have to be timing. There are a lot of different opportunities that are out there and I think timing and positioning is really the first key thing that you've got to look at when you look at a business opportunity or some sort of business venture. What is the timing of the service? What is the timing of the product?

When I first got into network marketing with Excel communications in the early 1990s, the timing was that long distance phone service had just been deregulated—it was perfect timing. When I got into the mortgage industry in 2001, it was perfect timing. In that five-and-a-half-year run, everybody was refinancing, buying, and flipping homes. It was timing, timing, timing.

Well, as I write this chapter, the mortgage industry and Real Estate industry is nowhere near where it used to be a few years ago. Right now, because of the economy being in such a downturn, a lot of people are looking for a plan B. This has posed an unprecedented time in the home-based business arena. More people than ever are turning to the Internet and some way to generate a true, sustainable income from the comfort of their home.

My second key component would be being in a leveraged income model; that's why I love direct sales and network marketing. Network marketing is the only arena you can actually get in and be horribly underpaid in the beginning (then paid about what you're worth) for the ability to be overpaid for the rest of your life. I think being in a leveraged income model like that is absolutely, unequivocally perfect, as I have witnessed the results firsthand. J. Paul Getty said it the best, "I would rather have 1 percent of one hundred people, than to have 100 percent of myself!" That goes back to listening to people who have what you want. J. Paul Getty was the first billionaire of this century! Leverage, leverage, leverage—network marketing and direct sales can offer that model to you.

The third thing I would say is representing an exclusive product. You don't want to be in the "me too" industry, looking like a peddler in the marketplace. There are particular products and services that are exclusive to certain companies and representing these types of products or services can be the difference in whether or not you make a significant income in your business. Standing out from the crowd will make a big difference in your success. Find companies that have products or services that are patented or proprietary to that company and watch your success soar. Or for that matter, invent a product or service that is proprietary and/or patented and be ready to take wheel barrows of cash to the bank.

The fourth thing would be the leadership. What is the leadership in your entity? What is the leadership of your particular company? Where has the leadership been? Where is the leadership positioned right now, and what is their future vision? You have to surround yourself with visionaries—people who can see the future and who can see through the forest.

WRIGHT

So how do you think the Internet has affected your success?

HARRIS

Wow. Well, the Internet has transformed my success dramatically. When I first jumped into the Internet full-time in January of 2006, I made a vow to myself that I had to learn everything I possibly could when it came down to Internet marketing. I attended numerous webinars, conferences calls, and have spent well over fifty thousand dollars on learning the power of the Internet and how to apply it in my business. I started studying people who were making over thirty thousand dollars per month on the Internet on a regular basis.

Well, because of this focus and determination, I can honestly say I don't know where I would be today if it wasn't for the Internet. I am now able to reach people across the globe in a matter of a millisecond. I have members on my team in countries like South Africa, Germany, London, and Canada all because of the Internet. I have learned how to build a list of buying prospects and because of this, one e-mail every week turns into thousands of dollars. I have been able to connect with many people I haven't seen or talked to in years because of the Internet. I can honestly say that, because of the Internet, I was able to write this book. Not only does my success on the Internet give me a story to tell, but I was able to ink this book deal due to one connection made on the Internet. When it comes to direct sales and network marketing I truly believe that if you don't use the Internet your success will take longer.

Just consider the facts:

- There are over 2.5 billion Internet users.
- The third largest Web site in the world is YouTube and it's free.
- The fifth largest Web site in the world is Facebook and it's free.

- People spend more time on the Internet than they do in front of the television.
- There are 100 new millionaires made every day due to the Internet.
- The Internet is the first place people go when they want information on any product and or service.

When you consider these facts, how can you dispute the power of the Internet? This is a trend that is never going away and the people who understand this will make a fortune. There is nothing that is out there that can be compared to what the Internet has meant to us a human race. And with that being said, if you want to see success faster in any business, learn Internet marketing!

WRIGHT

What advice would you give to future entrepreneurs who want to succeed in network marketing and direct sales?

HARRIS

Become a student of your craft. That is really the biggest thing that I can relate to anyone listening or anyone paying attention to this book—become a student of your craft. If you want to be a great Internet marketer, study great Internet marketers and what they do. If you want to be a great salesperson, study great salespeople and do what they do. Cut off the automatic income reducer, a.k.a., the television, and become a true student of your craft. This is actually a pretty easy task; however, most people just aren't willing to get out of their comfort zones to really accomplish it.

If you really want to become a student of your craft, read the next sentences very slowly. Fifteen years ago I was given a challenge by one of my mentors that changed my life forever. I am going to share this challenge with the whole world hoping that people will take me seriously and apply this in their life. I will tell you one thing, this challenge will make you uncomfortable, but it will be well worth it. Here we go:

Go around your home and count all of the televisions you have. Now multiply the amount of inches you have by the amount of televisions. This means that if you have four forty-two-inch screen televisions then you have one hundred and sixty-eight inches. Well, if you don't have at least one hundred and sixty-eight books, DVDs, CDs, or MP3s on your desired craft, then you need to get rid of a few televisions.

This exercise will show you how serious you are about your business. You will also learn why on my team we call the television the "automatic income reducer!" Focus on who you are becoming and hone your craft by reading, listening, and applying the teachings of the people you want to become like. I will tell you that if you want to be an actor, then watch a lot of television. If you want to be a game show host, watch a lot of television. If you want to be reporter, watch a lot of television. But if you want to be a true Internet marketer, direct sales professional, or network marketer, cut off the television and study the people you want to emulate.

I learned from the great Jim Rohn that if you want to increase your value to society, you must increase your education and bring more to the marketplace. So you really have to become a student of your craft; you have to read as much as you possibly can, you have to absorb yourself in audios and videos, you have to cut off the automatic income reducer. That is advice that I would give people because being a professional in network marketing and direct sales takes a certain dexterity. It takes a certain dexterity to be successful in an industry that has such a high failure rate; however the people who take it seriously receive so much abundance that it's scary. It's absolutely, unequivocally scary the abundance they receive just by focusing on their craft

WRIGHT

I know one of your favorite niches is prospecting. Why is that so important in direct sales and network marketing?

HARRIS

Prospecting is so important because it is your core task. This is the one skill that will separate you from everyone out there in your marketplace. We all know that money only comes from one place—people. So with that being said, you have to be good at communicating your message. You have to make prospecting second nature and part of your being.

Inside of network marketing no money is made unless there are new customers and/or new reps joining your organization. So if you aren't good at prospecting, no new reps or customers are walking in your door. And when that happens, your bank account will not look like you want it too.

Understanding human nature and personalities will ultimately help you become a master prospector. This is something that I do every day and I literally go through withdrawals when I don't get my prospecting in. When you understand that every prospect or customer typically has the same question or comment, you will be very good at prospecting because you will enjoy it. Predictability is power, and humans behave in predictable manners.

So when you become a great prospector, you learn to insert yourself in that equation—you are that person who is receiving versus giving. You're the person who actually understands that without prospecting you don't have a business and without having new blood in your direct sales or networking marketing business you don't have a true business. Without finding those five to ten people who would truly be responsible for the majority of your income, you don't have a business. This is why I teach prospecting so much and why I feel that prospecting is truly the life blood of any network marketing and direct sales business. This is a subject I regularly train people on (for more information visit www.CedrickHarris.com).

WRIGHT

Why is personal development so important in your arena, as well as in your life?

HARRIS

Personal development has allowed me to change my life dramatically. Just being in the direct sales arena and network marketing business for so long, one cannot become a professional without changing on the inside first.

Before anything changes on the outside, you must change first on the inside. So it's extremely important to focus on who you are becoming. One of the gentleman I follow a lot is Russell Simmons who is a mogul in the music industry. One of the things that I learned from him is to focus on the process and not on the prize. I learned the hard way that the prize is never what you thought it was going to be when you get it. There is always a bigger house, bigger bank account, better car, and more "toys" to buy. Learning how to connect with people better, learning to have a better positive attitude on life, learning why prospecting is so important, learning why you have to surround yourself with the people you want to become, and reading are all so important. All of those activities encompass personal development and without focusing on who you are becoming your journey will be empty and will lack a purpose.

WRIGHT

What one or two books have influenced your life the most?

HARRIS

Well, it's impossible not to include the greatest book on Earth—the Bible. I grew up in a very God fearing family. My mother was a Jehovah's Witness and I learned a lot about the Bible at a very, very young age and still learn from it to this day. I believe that the Bible is the best book ever written just from the stories that are given and the things that can be applied to regular everyday life. Everything you need to know is in that book. So I would definitely say that the Bible is the number one book.

The second one would be *The Greatest Secret in the World* by Og Mandino. One of my first outside sales managers, a gentleman by the name of Jim Haller, gave me this book when I was twenty years old. When I first started reading this book I had no idea of the affect that it would have in my life. This book encompasses the ten scrolls used by Benjamin Franklin to get rid of any bad habit in your life. He figured out that the only way to get rid of a bad habit was to replace it with a good one. In this book, you have to read one scroll every day three times a day—once in the morning, once in the afternoon, and once out loud right before you go to bed. Imbedding these scrolls in your mind every day for thirty days, your subconscious mind starts to follow the scrolls. It's an amazing journey and it's truthfully a book that I review on a regular basis. This book is a ten-month read because you have to practice all ten scrolls for thirty days each. I think that anyone looking to change his or her life in a big way has to read *The Greatest Secret in the World* by Og Mandino.

WRIGHT

So what type of sacrifices have you had to make in your life to achieve the level of success that you now have?

HARRIS

Wow, David, now that is a subject to discuss. The sacrifice that it has taken to get where I am today has been a lot. Just in the mortgage industry alone in the year 2003, I slept almost four hours a day every day for over a year. I had to work seven days a week, close to five years straight without a vacation. There were days I didn't even go home because I was so busy—I didn't have time to drive back and forth.

After my successful run in the mortgage industry, I began working in network marketing. The sacrifices I made there include long trips to numerous cities, the various hotels, and the road trips where I'd be gone for weeks at a time; but it's the nature of the business if you want true results.

However, it wouldn't be right if I didn't share how those sacrifices have helped my life. Now my family and I are able to do things we only thought about before. Because of those sacrifices we are able to travel to exotic destinations, own multiple homes, and live a lifestyle that we used to dream about.

So I've given up a lot when it comes to focusing and following my passion, but I would also say that it has been worth the sacrifice.

WRIGHT

At the end of the day, what do you want your legacy to be?

HARRIS

I want to be known as someone who truly influenced people to follow their passion. The great Jim Rohn said it the best. He said that if you want to be great, you truly have to find a way to influence many. I want people to know that no matter what obstacles they face, no matter what's in front of them, they can accomplish anything in life. I have been through so many trials and so many tribulations throughout my life and as a youngster that I feel extremely blessed now. It's an honor and privilege to be able to co-author this book, be a public speaker, multi-preneur and someone who influences many.

I learned from my coach and mentor, Jeffrey, never to die with any songs on the inside of you—never to take any songs to your grave. He tells me all the time, "Cedrick, so many people quietly tiptoe to their grave and arrive at their grave safely. Well, I don't want to quietly tiptoe to my grave—I want to give out every song I have in my body, whether it's through audio, DVDs, or in print. I want to give out all of my songs so my passions about life can really, truly live forever through other people by the way I've expressed myself." That's what I want my legacy to be David.

WRIGHT

Well, what a great conversation, Cedrick. I really appreciate all of this time you've spent with me this morning to answer these important questions. It seems that you are indeed an international recognized trainer in direct sales and network marketing. Perhaps some of this wisdom will rub off on some of our readers; at least that's my hope.

HARRIS

Very good; I hope so as well, David. I appreciate the time that you have given me and I enjoyed being able to share my thoughts about the direct sales and network marketing industry with you today.

WRIGHT

Today we've been talking with Cedrick Harris who is a trainer, a speaker, and an author in the network marketing and sales industry. His company Team Takeover Marketing has grown to over two thousand members worldwide in numerous countries.

Cedrick, thank you so much for being with us today on *Stepping Stones for Success.*

HARRIS

Thank you, David, I appreciate it.

CEDRICK HARRIS is an internationally recognized trainer, speaker, and author in the network marketing and direct sales industry. In 2006, after spending some very successful years in the mortgage industry as the president of marketing for a very large mortgage company, Cedrick decided to share his knowledge of the Internet with fellow entrepreneurs worldwide. His passion for direct sales and network marketing moved him to start Team Takeover Marketing LLC, a sales and marketing company focused on teaching entrepreneurs how to take over their lives both mentally and financially in the home-based business arena. His company has grown to over two thousand members worldwide, and Cedrick prides himself on teaching his philosophies on Internet marketing, closing skills, prospecting, and network marketing. He is considered one of the hottest rising superstars in the direct sales and in the network marketing arena.

CEDRICK HARRIS

5364 Ehrlich Rd #114
Tampa, Florida 33624
813-407-2743
CedrickHarris317@gmail.com
www.CedrickHarris.com

CHAPTER ELEVEN

Straight Talk

AN INTERVIEW WITH.... CASEY EBERHART

DAVID WRIGHT (WRIGHT)

By the age of five, Casey Eberhart began turning a profit as an entrepreneur. While friends grappled with kindergarten, Casey's series of small neighborhood companies honed skills that would set his career as a successful entrepreneur into motion.

Moving forward, Casey has found success in such diverse endeavors as managing an amusement park, working on an Oscar-winning film, and as a clothing manufacturer. As a top income earner and network marketer, his love for learning involves him in Toastmasters International and other professional organizations.

Casey lives his passion. He's achieved national recognition for a successful networking strategy he developed and now teaches. Casey's irresistible charisma, coupled with his commitment and support of others, foreshadows a prosperous future.

Casey, welcome to *Stepping Stones to Success*.

CASEY EBERHART (EBERHART)

Thank you so much, it's a pleasure to be here.

WRIGHT

Casey, in the speaking industry you've been referred to as an "edu-tainer." What's that?

EBERHART

An edu-tainer is one part educator and one part entertainer. One of the things that has always struck me at seminars and workshops is that the speakers are usually not very entertaining. Because of this, it's hard to grasp some of their concepts. I've really taken that to heart. Within the context of each of my seminars and workshops I deliver my material in a way that's also entertaining. By involving the audience and allowing them to become engaged in the conversation, overall participation goes up, retention goes up, and results are achieved. My goal is to take what might be perceived as a boring topic and spice it up by involving the audience.

One of the strategies I use is to make sure every single person who attends my workshops wears a nametag. This allows me to draw people into the conversation on a personal level, and people love to hear the sound of their own name.

Here is a summary of my concept of Edu-tainment: When I'm illustrating a specific topic, rather than in giving a long-winded speech in front of the room using a microphone and a PowerPoint presentation, I expand upon the topic within the context of the conversation. Using humor and stories and referring to people by name increases participation. I'll be discussing this in depth a little later.

WRIGHT

Who are your greatest business inspirations and why?

EBERHART

I love this question; it's a great question. Top leaders in any industry will usually say that those who've inspired them have laid the foundation for their success. These people are the backbones of great leaders, speakers, sales managers, or whatever.

I've personally been inspired by several people, and each has inspired me in different ways.

My first inspiration was my grandfather. He was a true entrepreneur. Having grown up during the depression, he learned how to conserve, collecting everything from wheat pennies to Model T's. He would collect pens whenever he visited a bank, thinking that those pens might someday be valuable if the bank went out of business. He viewed them as an investment.

My grandfather owned an antique store in an old garage in Colorado. It was on a vacation there at the age of five when I felt my first pulse of entrepreneurial spirit. My grandfather really lifted that up in me. I remember him specifically teaching me what a garage sale was and how important it was to treat customers right—to give them a good value.

My vacation ended, but I took that spark of inspiration back with me to my home in Seattle. Shortly after my return home, I made "Garage Sale" signs and, in the middle of the night, I stapled them to all the telephone poles in the neighborhood. The next morning, I put out little picnic benches piled high with my parents' belongings. When I was ready, I opened up the garage doors and started selling stuff. I never bothered to tell my parents what I was doing—I just did it. I don't think they were even aware that I knew what a garage sale was. I remember very clearly my mom opening the door to a garage full of people at about seven in the morning, as I sold their chainsaw for a quarter!

The *lesson in the lesson* was about providing value to the customer. That very first spark of inspiration from my grandfather was huge for me. Learning what a sale was, the exchange of dollars for value, and how to treat people paved the way for my success in business.

Robert Kiyosaki, tried and true entrepreneur, was also a source of inspiration. I come from a similar background. My story begins with my best friend from childhood, Brian Ruffo. We shared a lot of life experiences growing up together, and our friendship has endured through the years. Brian's father was a high level executive of a big-time, publicly traded company. Frank Ruffo was very new school in his interpretation of entrepreneurialism. As a veterinarian, my own dad is also a successful entrepreneur, following a more conservative, *old school* way of doing business. The Robert Kiyosaki material reminds me to keep moving toward the new future of entrepreneurialism while keeping old-school values intact.

I would never have arrived at this point in my life without the support of a couple of coaches—Patricia McDade, who owned and created The Consulting Alliance, and my personal coach, Yvonne Teruya. They, along with the rest of the Consulting Alliance staff, have propelled me into a stratosphere of success I would never have imagined possible. They were the ones who introduced terms like *context* and *conversation* into my vocabulary. I've always been an entrepreneur, but with the help with both Patricia and Yvonne I've been able to get out of my own way and allow space to create my own destiny. I've learned to accept things as they come. Life works!

Todd Falcone, a speaker, trainer, and coach in the area of network marketing taught me the value of (and I'll steal his phrase here) *keeping my foot on the gas.* When you're building a business, whether it's network marketing or traditional business, a veterinarian or a beer distributorship for that matter, *keeping your foot on the gas* at all times will propel your sales, your relationships, and ultimately fuel your success.

The next couple of people fall under the category of: *find some people who have what you want, and develop friendships with them. And then engage them as mentors.* Jordan Adler, a very close personal friend of mine, just wrote an amazing book on network marketing called *Beach Money,* available at www.beachmoney.com. All the profits from *Beach Money* go to *Kiva.* Jordan is an amazing teacher in the area of relationship development. I've always been really good with developing relationships; I consider myself a connector in business. But Jordan's book, his friendship, and mentorship have really honed that skill into something valuable.

Jordan introduced me to an amazing entrepreneur by the name of Kody Bateman, the Founder and CEO of a company called SendOutCards. This happens to be a company that I'm very heavily involved with. Kody provided the space for a transformational shift in how I view business. It's actually kind of a funny story.

I became involved with SendOutCards, a thriving new company that helps people keep in touch, express gratitude, and reach out to others through greeting cards. My goal was to produce a direct mail piece for an equipment rental company I owned. My intention was to send greeting cards to my clients, advertising my products and services. I was really not having that much success. I went to hear Kody speak, not because I wanted to find out what he had to say, but because I wanted to meet other businesspeople who were using SendOutCards to generate more business. From the audience I heard Kody say a phrase that will forever change my life. Whenever I'm about get ready to say the phrase I actually get goose bumps. It's literally happening right now as we're talking. That phrase is: *Appreciation will win out over self-promotion every single time.*

In that split second, I shifted. It became clear to me that rather than teaching people how to market and advertise themselves, as the old school college education programs teach, it's really about connecting with people. It's about appreciating them for who they are, and the services/products they provide.

SendOutCards provides the mechanics of making things happen. It's about saying to a person, *Thank you. I appreciate everything that you have done for me.* Or, *Please allow me to send this referral on to you. If there's anything I can do for you, please call me and let me know. I'm more than happy to help.*

That sounds a heck of a lot better and does a lot more for the recipient than saying, "*Save 30 percent next time you call Atomic Production Supplies. We want to rent you more of our equipment.*"

It's a very big difference. No matter what business people are in, it's really about connectivity in the marketplace. Connectivity comes from building and nurturing relationships.

WRIGHT

Casey, what were the major turning points in your life and in what ways did they influence your business?

EBERHART

I talked about the first major turning point in my life when I illustrated how my grandfather taught me the value of customer relationship skills though the garage sale concept. That was a massive turning point.

The second may sound a bit negative at first, but I'm going to flip it to a positive. A few years ago, I went against my gut instinct and bought a clothing manufacturing business. Some would call it a sweatshop, but I was in marketing so it was a "*perspiration salon.*" We had one hundred and twenty employees and were making about six thousand pair of pants a day. My partner, Brandon Vukelich, and I were both miserable. There was nothing about that particular business I enjoyed except being able to work with my partner. Truth be told, if it had not been for Brandon, I don't know if we'd be having this conversation today.

Purchasing that business was the first time I really went against my gut instinct. But it was a positive experience in that I learned the importance of going with your gut. You really have to go where your heart is, and my heart has always been with connecting people, helping them build relationships and businesses, and having an amazingly awesome time while doing it. It became very clear to me that sitting behind a desk watching over people with a magnifying glass in a negative environment snuffed out the flame of my soul.

At the time, I was also working SendOutCards. That was the only thing providing any fun in my life. I walked away from the perspiration salon, and when I say I lost a lot of money in that business (I won't give you the exact figure), it was pretty much everything I'd built up to that point in my life, with the exception of the car I drove and the house I lived in. From that point forward I had to rebuild. Finding my passion and helping people get ahead in what they were doing—I wouldn't trade that experience for anything in the world.

The third and final turning point came in that tiny workshop room in Salt Lake City, hearing Kody Bateman utter the phrase, *Appreciation will win out over self-promotion every single time.* I cannot tell you how that changed my life! I've become quite good friends with Kody and his family and I don't think at the time he understood the affect that phrase might have had on somebody in his audience. Because of this, when I speak, I always teach that you have no idea as a speaker or a presenter, an employee, a boss, or as a guy on Facebook or Twitter, how something you say from a pulpit or a soapbox or a podium might affect somebody. That to me is really inspiring.

WRIGHT

Many people see *you* as an inspiration, Casey. What are they talking about?

EBERHART

David, I have absolutely no idea. Seriously, I get that a lot and although it's flattering, I certainly don't view myself as an inspiration. Perhaps people feel this way *because* I don't view myself as an inspiration. I try to approach everything with zero ego.

I've discovered that simply appreciating people and showing it increases sales. Increasing sales builds relationships and creates a new paradigm for doing business. I believe in my heart of hearts that we get back what we send out. A common theme in our SendOutCards family is that if we send out negative energy to the world, we're going to get it back about tenfold. If the vast majority of what we take in on a daily basis is negative, it perpetuates cycle of negativity. And the same goes for positive energy. So I make it a goal to introduce the concept of doing something good for somebody every day.

I'm the goofball who walks down the street with a pocket full of quarters, and secretly, without anybody knowing it, if I see somebody's parking meter out of time, I'll put a quarter on it. I'm not looking for somebody to congratulate me or pat me on the back; I just want to help someone avoid a bad day. If I know somebody's birthday is coming up, for me sending them a birthday card is a no-brainer. It's a dollar!

I enjoy helping others look at a life through a different set of lenses. If everybody did something for three strangers every day, imagine how the world would shift. We'd create a completely different paradigm; it would be absolutely awesome.

WRIGHT

Leaders often encounter obstacles, and overcoming these obstacles helps make them good leaders. Would you tell our leaders about some of your greatest challenges and how you overcame them?

EBERHART

I'll use the fashion business as a good example to illustrate. Do you remember that I said this was one of my biggest struggles? It was a challenge on so many different levels; one of which was dealing with different cultures. I live in Los Angeles right now, a pretty diverse culture in and of itself, but managing the cultural dynamics in my perspiration salon was a real struggle.

I didn't enjoy what I was doing. I was working in an industry that didn't reflect the values I integrated and operated by in business. It wasn't about good customer service and fair business dealings. It was about driving down the price and seeing who could take advantage of whom the fastest. That's who won the game. This was an entirely negative experience and it took me about a year (and losing a ton of money) to realize the need for an internal paradigm shift. It wasn't even the industry itself but the paradigm that I was operating under.

Years ago, I had the privilege of being entrusted with managing an amusement and water park. I was responsible for a lot of money rolling through the turnstiles of that park at a really young age. This was a busy park and, as with any business, there were occasional complaints. Most issues were easily remedied, but every now and then a customer wanted to speak to the boss. The chain of command went something like this: We had employees, and their immediate supervisors (leads), who were accountable to department managers. The next level of command consisted of area managers, and if an issue was still unresolved, I was called. I was the final point of contact in that long line.

Just imagine. By the time I was brought into the conversation, the customer was pretty upset (an understatement). Let's put it this way, most of the time, I was flanked by police officers when I went to meet with the customer.

The lessons taught by my granddad so long ago were still anchored firmly in place. I remember that I always had the customer in mind. I always put myself in his or her place. But it was really interesting—no matter how much I did or how hard I tried to help, I couldn't get past the age thing. I was twenty-two or twenty-three years old and dealing with people who were very hostile, very angry, and who could not get in their head that a twenty-three-year-old kid was the manager and had the final say.

Working to get past that, I really had to take stock of the issue—my age. I really had to see beyond this and look at how to communicate with the customer. That obstacle, sometimes insurmountable, became easier to deal with as I learned the value of listening rather than talking. Todd Falcone always says, you have two ears and one mouth. There's a reason. When you listen to anyone—a customer, a consumer, the person on the other side of the deal—and if you listen long enough, you'll understand what he or she actually wants or expects. Listening gives you a much better opportunity to give customers what they want without compromising. It's nothing more than creating win-wins.

The truth is, I don't view any of these examples as obstacles, but as challenges. Once I'm challenged, I seek out possible solutions. I'm determined to find a way through to the other side.

WRIGHT

You've said many times that your primary goal is to help businesspeople and entrepreneurs improve their bottom line, but you've also designed a powerful, easy-to-learn system for creating income-generating relationships at networking events. Would you give us a quick teaser?

EBERHART

Absolutely; I love this. I see it as one of the biggest stumbling blocks facing people at networking events. These events are designed to help people grow their businesses by meeting others and building their networks. But most people attend these events and don't know what to do. They go without a specific goal in mind. I'll use chamber of commerce events as an example, but feel free to consider Kiwanis, Lions, BNI, or any other kind of networking group.

I've developed a simple strategy that people can use with any networking opportunity. I call the system *Finding the Yappers*. Let me expand on that. In order to get the most value from a networking event, it's essential to have a plan.

One of the formulas I've had great success with is to arrive a little early. I stand off to the side and observe the room. My goal is to meet five people and five people only. Here are the five people I'm going to meet and introduce myself to: First, I introduce myself to the presenter or speaker. Sometimes this will be a sponsor—somebody who will be in front of the room at some point. Meeting this person before he or she goes on stage increases my opportunity for exposure. Any attention they give me from the front of the room is going to be invaluable;

it's validating. I make sure presenters know my name and I try to sit in the front. If they start to use examples and I'm the only person in the chamber they've met, the likelihood is greater that I'll be used as the example.

Next, I make the acquaintance of the organization's president. For example, at a chamber of commerce meeting, it might be the executive director or CEO. Depending on the group, it may be the membership director. (One of the first things I did with a chamber I'm involved with was to volunteer in the office. I can't tell you how much business I have received from becoming friends with people who run the organization.)

The final three people are the most important. Those are the Yappers. The Yappers are guys and gals who are loud and maybe even a little bit obnoxious, but they're standing there holding court. They have five or six people standing around them. People are attracted to them. They're a bit more boisterous, and everybody knows them. These folks may not be doing a lot of business, but everybody knows them. They're comedians, probably the "class clowns." Yappers are easy to pick out when you begin to watch for them. I would be considered a Yapper. Kay Wallace, my friend and business partner in www.tools2connect.com, would also be considered a Yapper.

My objective is to spend about five to ten minutes with each of these five key people. Mathematically that's about an hour. Then I take those five people and I introduce two or three couples of those, so maybe the executive director to one of the Yappers, maybe another Yapper to another Yapper, maybe the speaker to a Yapper.

It goes something like this:

"Hey Jen, I want you to meet Kay, and Kay, I want you to meet Jen. I don't know how you would work together, but I'm sure you'll find a way because I just vibe well with your personalities."

And then, I turn around and leave. The reason I leave is because the only thing that those two people have in common in that exact second is me.

"So how do *you* know Casey?"

"Oh, I don't know. I just met him ten minutes ago. He's doing this introduction thing, I kind of like it. It's cool."

Then they go on and talk between themselves and I'm out of the equation. That's okay with me. I do that a couple of times and then I leave. I don't stick around. I don't make it a goal of handing out my business cards—I'm actually one of the few people who don't take business cards to a networking event. I don't want people to think I have *commission breath*. I don't want to walk into an event and sell my product to a hundred and fifty people who are there trying to sell their products to a hundred and fifty people who are not buying because they're trying to sell their product to a hundred and fifty people. I just go with my two ears and listen and introduce people.

Now here's the key. Once I leave the event, I'm going to send a card or an e-mail or give a phone call to all five of those people. I might try to set up coffee with Kay if it will work and if she has the time, but it's more important with me to follow up with her just to say, *"Hey, it was great to meet you; I loved getting to know you. I'd love to be able to get to know you better and see how I can throw you some business, let's get together for coffee [or whatever]."*

The result of an attempt to contact is unimportant. If I send Kay a greeting card or *nice to meet you* card or an e-mail and she doesn't respond, I'm totally okay with it. As my grandfather always said, *"We've got to keep a stiff upper lip."* Here's where the value is: When I show up next month at the exact same event and I walk into a room where Kay is holding court as one of the Yappers, it's likely that she'll spot me and say, "Oh, my gosh, Casey! Thank you so much for the e-mail" or "Thank you so much for the brownies" or "Thank you so much for the phone call!"

"I'm sorry we didn't get caught up—"

What has she just done? She's just validated me in front of everyone she's holding court for currently. I've now become somebody people want to get to know. That's where the relationship starts.

WRIGHT

That's a great plan.

As an edu-tainer, you've had a profound effect on the way people in your network do business, which ultimately will be your legacy. How else would you like to be remembered?

EBERHART

That's another question I get asked quite often. How I'm remembered isn't really important to me. What's really important to me is that I make and leave the world a better place than when I got here.

Here's how I see things. When my life on this Earth is done and I lay down to take a dirt nap (as I like to call it), if I've done my job, I've made the world a better place. I look at my entire life as a dash. I've heard other people talk about this but I really take it to heart.

My grandmother recently passed away, and I had the opportunity to walk around the cemetery where she was buried. On each headstone was an acknowledgement of somebody's life. From his or her birth to the year of the person's death, the entire life of that person was literally represented by a dash, for example: 1972–2009. All of the things the person did in between—the jobs held, the families the person created, the adventures experienced—were all represented by that one little dash.

It's always been my hope and desire to make my dash as thick and full as possible.

Kody Bateman introduced so many things into my life. One of them was the practice of putting affirmations on three by five cards and carrying them in my pocket. As we speak, in my wallet, I literally have a three by five card that says, *I am making my dash as thick and as full as possible.* That's how I rule and run my life. If I can help others make their dashes thicker and fuller, then I've done my job. It's not really important to me how I'm remembered, but that the world is a better place than when I got here.

WRIGHT

You've got some great stories about your adventures as a kid. Let's go back and talk about a few of them. Can you remember the first time you acted on the entrepreneurial blood coursing through your veins?

EBERHART

The answer to that goes back to my granddad's garage sale story (I *love* that story). I grew up with very cool parents. I never wanted for anything. But I can remember as a kid my mother's designer choices for my school clothes and my own choices differed. So, I took hold of that entrepreneurial spirit as a kid and built businesses so I could afford to buy my own school clothes and not have to wear the stiff pants or the scratchy-elbowed t-shirts my mother preferred. I wanted to wear what the cool kids wore.

I clearly remember doing things like having Hot Wheels races, where I charged the kids to race their cars. I got little trophies and rented lawn chairs from the neighbors. When people came to watch the Hot Wheels races, I basically sold them a ticket to sit in their own chair.

I can remember my first true company. My parents had this beautiful bank of ivy. One night a bunch of the neighborhood parents were over. Everyone was commenting on how beautiful the ivy was. So I went to H & H in Puyallup, Washington, and I bought this stuff you could stick a trimming in and it would actually grow roots. I started a company called *Grow It Green Nursery* in my parents' greenhouse. I grew ivy starts and sold that ivy back to all the neighborhood residents.

I grew up during the eighties. One Christmas in particular, Cabbage Patch Dolls were huge. It was like the Tickle Me Elmo—if you didn't get a Cabbage Patch Kid you were not cool. At the same time there was a commercial on television for a dog treat called Snausages. This little cartoon dog would yap, "Snausages! Snausages!" I don't know where it came from but I had this brilliant idea that if I could combine those two concepts I was on to a billion dollar enterprise.

First, I paid the kids in the neighborhood fifty cents each to steal their moms' pantyhose and bring them to me. Then I set up a little assembly line. I cut the panty hose off at the knees and stuffed them full of cotton. I sewed eyes on and a little mouth. I stuck them in a shoebox with some Easter grass. I wrapped the whole thing in cellophane with an adoption certificate and sold *Snausage Patch Kids.* Sales didn't go very well. I also got in quite a bit of trouble when I tried to sell a Snausage Patch Kid to parents we had stolen pantyhose from. But for me it was the concept rather than the execution.

I always get the biggest kick out of telling this next story. It's an awesome example of when entrepreneurialism meets opportunity. This experience gave me confidence, in that I don't think like most people. I always try to go unconventional. The term *out of the box thinking* has become cliché in my opinion, but it's a matter of thinking differently and from a much bigger picture than a small picture.

I had just started seventh grade at Edgemont Junior High School when Price Savers Store (similar to Costco or Sam's Club) opened up in our neighborhood. Items were sold in cases or large quantities. I thought it was so cool that you could buy boxes of candy as you could at the grocery stores but you didn't have to pay nearly as much as the grocery store charged. So I bought a couple of boxes of candy and stuffed them into my locker at school. I was just going to eat the candy myself but kids started wanting to buy it. So I started selling candy out of my locker between classes. Then, as any entrepreneur would, I went a little further. I carried my books on my back all day and turned my locker into coolest candy store you've ever seen. I'm sure nobody has beaten it today. I mean it was *cool.* Between and often during classes I would sell candy. I skipped lunch. I would just sell candy.

I sold Tootsie Pops (remember Tootsie Pops?). There was this rumor that if you got one with an Indian shooting a star it meant something. Well, I sold so many of those it was ridiculous. It wasn't long before I got called down to Mr.

McKamey's office, as any kid who was creating litter on the floor of a school should be. Mr. McKamey sat me down and looked me straight in the eye.

"Listen, Casey, if you sell that candy and I find one more wrapper or one more stick on the floor of this school, you're going to stay after and you're going to sweep the whole school!"

Now, I'm sitting there figuring I had a little bit of an *in* because my mother, a junior high school principal, and Mr. McKamey traveled in the same professional circle. She designed high schools and junior high schools, and was very well known within the education system.

So I'm striving to give Mr. McKamey a little leeway to avoid being suspended on the spot, but I sat right there at that instant and thought, *What's this guy saying?* What I had heard was, "If I find litter on the floor you're going to stay after school and sweep the floor."

I can tell you, David, that I sat and I questioned him five or six times.

"Mr. McKamey, so what you're saying, if I understand you, is that if you find wrappers on the floor I'm going to have to stay after and sweep the floor?"

All he would've had to tell me was I couldn't sell candy anymore, but he didn't.

He just said, "Yes."

I remember it very specifically. As I was getting up, the lunch bell rang so the hall flooded with kids. I mean they were just packed right outside Mr. McKamey's office as they were coming out of classes going to lunch.

I said, "Okay, great. I got it."

I stood up. I literally did not even break the plane of the office door before I screamed at the top of my lungs to the entire student body that I was having a half price sale on Tootsie Pops and that it was, *Throw Your Tootsie Pop Wrapper On The Floor* Day.

I stayed after school every day in seventh grade and swept the school floor for forty-five minutes each day. I made about $50 a day selling candy, so my calculation was that this amounted to $50 an hour. I could still skateboard with my buddies afterward but I stayed after school and swept the floor because I knew that it was making me money, and I had more money than any kid I knew.

WRIGHT

Sounds like your youthful entrepreneurial ventures over the years were likely a springboard for the business that you started as an adult.

Among other things, you worked on an Oscar-winning movie, manufactured clothing, and today you're also making a significant contribution in the network marketing industry. What was the course of events that led you to your success?

EBERHART

When I was given the opportunity to work at the amusement park it really taught me a valuable lesson: *It's all about relationships.* It doesn't matter if I work for an amusement park or on feature films.

I had a great run working in Hollywood. I actually moved from Washington to Los Angeles to work in the movie business. I had the great fortune of working on a movie that won all types of awards, including Best Picture of the Year.

In some ways it was such a high point, but then I got sick of making other people millions and millions of dollars and not being rewarded for that effort. So I started an equipment rental company, renting back equipment to the friends I used to hire in the film business. Some of my best friends came from the film business, but again I wasn't really into helping studios and other people make millions of dollars. I like to be paid on my performance. I'm confident in my performance, and I'm okay at making what I'm worth so long as it's in proportion to what I produce.

Through my equipment rental company, we introduced the notion that *Appreciation wins out over self-promotion every time,* and I was able to use those mechanics to propel the company to fascinating levels. In about three years we were the third largest rental company in the entire Los Angeles marketplace. That's when we sold.

This transaction hurled me directly into the fashion business. As I've said, the fashion business, although not the best experience, allowed me to discover my passion—connecting people and building relationships one at a time.

It was then when I got involved in network marketing. Here was an industry that would allow me to help people change the course of their lives by teaching them how to put a little extra money (or a *lot* of extra money) in their pockets. I saw the industry of network marketing as this really cool thing to help people change the financial quality of their lives. If you can offer people a vehicle to make changes in a way that is fun and easy, and a mechanism by which you are paid for your own performance and the performance of the people you help, to me that's the golden combination.

I realize that network marketing isn't for everyone. It really depends on who you are and who you want to become. It's about educating people that, with a little effort and being paid for your own performance network marketing, creates way more security than even the highest paying job at the biggest Fortune 500 company.

I have so many friends whose "secure job that they've been at fifteen years" where they "are a top producer in their industry" has left them sitting around their house asking, what do I do next?

So I just love it. There is nothing about network marketing that I don't find fascinatingly awesome.

WRIGHT

What do you think is the biggest challenge facing the entrepreneur in the not so distant future?

EBERHART

Where do I start?

I think the biggest challenge, not only facing the entrepreneur, but also the microprenuer, the soloprenuer, the momprenuer, all the way to Fortune 500 companies is very simple. It's remaining stuck in an old paradigm and in not looking to the future where new relationships are forged.

When I listen to what some contemporary consultants present and pitch, it strikes me as being old school. I've started teaching classes in social media because that's the direction we're going in today's marketplace. Even large corporations are starting to come on board with social media because they've seen what a guy like me can create.

The challenge for most people is in discerning whether what they've been doing is still working. Are they allowing themselves even a tiny bit of an opening to look at something new? I understand that not everybody understands computers or understands social media or understands relationship marketing. But it's closed-mindedness that causes a person to say, to say, "My way is working and I'm not going to change."

With that attitude, they'd better have a backup plan, because the new guy and the younger generation are steamrolling forward with new concepts and innovations that we've never seen before. That's exciting! It's unfortunate that there are some big companies in our current marketplace that are going under because they haven't been able to embrace the idea that there are new concepts coming down the pipeline.

WRIGHT

Of course the world is moving swiftly from Web and e-mail to the next level of technology — social media marketing and blogging. What are your thoughts about such platforms as Twitter, Facebook, or LinkedIn?

EBERHART

Technology is always evolving. Social media outlets are opening people to relationships all over the world. Whether it's Facebook or LinkedIn or twitter or Plaxo or blogging, for that matter, it's all about expanding your relationship reach. It's about sorting through a wide funnel of people and sifting it down into a narrow funnel that can create actual leads and valuable relationships.

Right now Twitter is really big. A couple of months ago, CNN and Ashton Kutcher had a contest to see who could hit a million followers on Twitter. Today, both of those parties are up over two million followers. And Twitter is just a little micro-blog that allows one hundred and forty characters to answer a question: What are you doing? People can follow your little microblog and that microblog can be anything from "go to this link" to "I just woke up and had a great cup of coffee."

I read an article about CNN and why they put so much press time into building that contest. The result was that at any given point in time, CNN can go on their Twitter account and put out a microblog of a breaking story (we call them tweets) and more people will see that microblog entry in a split second than at any point of the day. That way, more people will be watching CNN. To me that's a very powerful tool for building relationships.

I started blogging about two years ago. My blog is not designed to sell anything. There might be a couple of things I recommend, maybe a book, but it's not really designed to sell anything. My blog is designed to allow the reader to get to know me. I don't throw out, *buy my stuff, buy my stuff,* and have *"commission breath."* Again, it goes back to the same concept as that of a chamber of commerce event. If you try to hock a hundred products to people who don't want to buy because they're selling their own stuff, you're at an impasse. I attract people into my business rather than try to go out and market to them.

So if I go on Twitter and say, "Hey gang, I just wrote a new blog post at TheIdealNetworker.com," and hit the send button, I can command about a thousand people at any given spot and time to go to that blog and read what I have to say.

I use social media as a way for people to get to know who I am. I allow them to see a day in the life of me, and if that's okay with them and it's something they like and enjoy, then they're going to want to know what I do. That's why it's really important in the social media marketplace to brand yourself. I pass out evaluation forms at my social media classes. More often than not, people comment that the best information they received was my five rules of social media.

I hadn't planned to talk about this, but let me give you my five quick tips to increase the likelihood that your sales funnel of potential clients will expand rather than shrink. Here are my five quick tips:

No sports. I never talk about sports in social media, because if I like one team and somebody else likes another team, I've created an adverse relationship right from the get-go.

No politics. Approximately, in our day and age, half the country believes one thing, and half the country believes the exact opposite. So if I go on there and start pitching my political beliefs, I would be naïve to think that the people on the other side of the issues are going to want to jump on and do business with me.

- I don't talk religion.
- I don't talk sex.
- I don't talk anything negative.

Some people use social media as a platform to rant about bad customer service they received somewhere or that they're having a bad day. Some people even complain that their husband isn't treating them well or that their wife is on their nerves. I don't ever talk about those things. Remember: You get back what you send out, tenfold. If you're sending out a negative vibe, you're going to get it back. So in the social media realm, write your negative thoughts in a diary, don't put them on the Internet for everybody to read. At the very least, open a separate account where nobody knows it's you.

Blogging, social media, video casting—these prove that things are moving to a technology that allows us to communicate with masses of people and funnel them down to the people who really want to design and build relationships with us.

I view myself as a sifter and a sorter and as a talent scout. That's really all I'm doing. I'm looking for people who want to do business with me based on knowing a little bit about me based on what I put out into the world.

WRIGHT

Would you give us an example of what you do put on your blog?

EBERHART

I'm a very practical guy. Even though I can talk a little bit of theory, I like to give people absolute nuts and bolts. I'll give you a good example. On my blog I wrote about a lady I came in contact with recently. She sells a drink designed to help people lose weight and provide a massive amount of energy. Her whole pitch was that this juice gives you massive energy. Well, she was without a doubt the most lethargic, boring, mean spirited, negative person I'd ever met. It was interesting because this was totally contrary to how she presented her product.

"Hi, my name is [we'll call her Sue], *I think this energy drink is fantastic."* She said it with no energy whatsoever.

So I inquired, *"Well, Sue, how long have you been selling this juice?"* I was thinking that she was obviously pretty new because she has no energy for a product that is supposed to sell energy.

She told me, *"Three years."*

Three years? That was an immediate deal-killer.

So one of the things I wrote in my blog was: "Look, you've got to live what you sell. For me, I love people, I love connecting people, I love making people feel important, and I love making people feel special. My product is something that I love. I use it every day, and I enjoy sharing it with others." Again, this goes back to making the world a better place if people want to increase their network.

I'm that annoying guy who always sits in the middle seat on an airplane. I have the best assistant in the world, Christina, and whenever she books my air travel she makes sure the trip has as many legs as possible—pretty much the opposite of what many people do. Here's my strategy: Although it may take me three stopovers to arrive at my destination, I'm seated between two different people on each leg. They're a captive audience! During the flight, I have an opportunity to find out who they are as people and discover how I might be able to help them. All in all, I have access to six different people and, assuming each knows approximately two hundred and fifty people, I have potentially increased my network quite a bit.

A second example I like to use illustrates the value of creating opportunities to meet new people.

Meeting just one new person a day can, over the course of many months, help you build a huge network. If you meet one person a day and each person knows two hundred and fifty people, by the end of the year, you've potentially increased your network by tens of thousands of people. I calculated this on a blog post—you now have access to 92,500 people. If you really get to know each individual and find out what makes him or her tick, you'll eventually find a way to help each one.

These are the nuts and bolts, real-life examples I use when I'm in front of a room or posting on the blog.

WRIGHT

So what benefits do you offer clients who work with you?

EBERHART

None! (Just joking.) When I tell people what benefits they're going to get from working with me, I really stress that my focus is helping them build whatever business they're in. I do that with complete nuts and bolts. I do that by really getting to know them and listening to what their needs are and because I consider myself a connector. I'm hoping that throughout this interview you got an idea that I'm fairly well connected. There are very few people I can't in a split second generate leads for, and so somebody working with me benefits from being introduced to people who can actually put dollars in their pocket.

I'll give you a quick example. I was teaching a social media class, and there was a lady in the front row with her arms folded. She was negative the whole time, saying *this is stupid, I don't understand why I'm here*. I asked her what she did. She happened to sell advertising on the back of Catholic church newsletters—a very specific niche. This lady couldn't understand why in a class on social media she was learning how to generate relationships with people. She didn't see the value or the need. So in front of the whole class, I literally got on my Twitter account and said, "Hey I have this lady I'd love to try to help out. I'd love to find her a couple of leads. Does anybody ever buy advertising on the back of Catholic church newsletters?" Within three minutes I had five to seven leads from people who wanted to contact her.

So a benefit of working with me is really the ability to start seeing things from a different perspective. You're also going to meet some people who are in my network because I'm always trying to connect people. You're going to be educated on how to be a connector.

WRIGHT

So is there anything else you would like to share with our readers?

EBERHART

Well, David, I really appreciate you and I also want to acknowledge everybody in my network. I want to acknowledge my assistant Christina (www.vaagogo.com) without whom I would be a mess. One of my business partners, Kay Wallace, who has partnered with me in Tools2Connect.com, really gives me a little kick when I need it. She may call it a boost, but I call it a kick. I appreciate my personal business coach, Yvonne. Without Yvonne I still might be making pants.

So many people have supported me over the years. I'd like to begin by thanking the coolest family ever—Mom and Dad, Chad, Des, Hunter, and Bridger Dean, without whom this journey would not be nearly as meaningful. Special thanks to David Royer for being there. To Kody, Jodi, Michelle, and Kris Bateman—thank you! Without your contribution to my life I might also still be making pants. I'd like to acknowledge my grandparents, Vernon and Laveta Eberhart, along with my best-friend-in-law, Jaime Vukelich. Special thanks go to Brian Ruffo, to Whitney Jensen, Leann McFalls, and Megan Drescher. Thank you to Barb and Eric Clemmons, to Bob Crisp (for teaching me the right way), to Bita, and to all of the current and future members of Team Appreciation Nation. Thanks to Judith Cassis, successmadesimpleteleseminars.com for always making me sound awesome.

I want to acknowledge everyone reading this material. Today, with the Internet and all of the great leaders in our society, there are so many options. I hope that I've been able to contribute something that will improve your life or the way you do business. I appreciate your listening to my stories and my experiences and hope that you're more motivated to connect with others, to build your business by cultivating relationships, and make your dash thick and full as possible. I hope that someday when you look back over your life, you'll know your being here made a difference, and the world is a better place because of your contributions.

WRIGHT

Well, what a great conversation, Casey. I really appreciate all the time you've taken with me today to answer these questions. It's absolutely been not only enjoyable but it's been educational. I've taken notes here copiously.

EBERHART

And I really appreciate it David. I'd just like to end by giving my favorite six-word quote. Sun Tzu, Chinese general and author (500–320 BC), said, "Opportunities multiply as they are seized."

WRIGHT

Great words to end this conversation. Today we've been talking with Casey Eberhart. Casey is an accomplished network marketer who has a love for learning. He lives his passion, as we have found out today. Casey has achieved national recognition for a networking strategy that he not only developed but now teaches.

Casey, thank you so much for being with us today on *Stepping Stones to Success.*

EBERHART

And thank you, David, for having me.

By the age of five, Casey Eberhart began turning a profit as an entrepreneur While friends grappled with kindergarten, Casey's series of small neighborhood companies honed skills that would set his career as a successful entrepreneur into motion.

Moving forward, Casey has found success in such diverse endeavors as managing an amusement park, working on an Oscar-winning film, and as a clothing manufacturer. As a top income earner and network marketer, his love for learning involves him in Toastmasters International and other professional organizations.

Casey lives his passion. He's achieved national recognition for a successful networking strategy he developed and now teaches. Casey's irresistible charisma, coupled with his commitment and support of others, foreshadows a prosperous future.

CASEY EBERHART
The Ideal Networker
5848 Hazeltine, Ave #2
Valley Glen, CA 91404
310.3454.9019
casey@thedealnetworker.com
www.theidealnetworker.com

NOTES

NOTES